Accumula 4

STUDENT BOOK

T0283639

JUMP Math
One Yonge Street, Suite 1014
Toronto, Ontario M5E 1E5
Canada
www.jumpmath.org

Writers: Dr. John Mighton, Dr. Sindi Sabourin, Dr. Anna Klebanov, Dr. Sohrab Rahbar, Julie Lorinc
Editors: Natalie Francis, Dimitra Chronopoulos, Debbie Davies-Wright, Ewa Krynski
Layout and Illustrations: Linh Lam, Gabriella Kerr
Cover Design: Sunday Lek
Cover Photograph: © Olga_Ionina/Shutterstock
ISBN 978-1-77395-296-3

First printing January 2024

Parts of this material were first published in 2013 in AP Book 4.1, US edition (978-1-927457-12-2) and AP Book 4.2, US edition (978-1-927457-13-9).

Printed and bound in Canada

Welcome to JUMP Math!

Entering the world of JUMP Math means believing that every learner has the capacity to be fully numerate and love math.

The **JUMP Math Accumula Student Book** is the companion to the **JUMP Math Accumula** supplementary resource for Grades 1 to 8, which is designed to strengthen foundational math knowledge and prepare all students for success in understanding math problems at grade level. This book provides opportunities for students to consolidate learning by exploring important math concepts through independent practice.

Unique Evidence-Based Approach and Resources

JUMP Math's unique approach, Kindergarten to Grade 8 resources, and professional learning for teachers have been producing positive learning outcomes for children and teachers in classrooms in Canada, the United States, and other countries for over 20 years. Our resources are aligned with the science on how children's brains learn best and have been demonstrated through studies to greatly improve problem solving, computation, and fluency skills. (See our research at **jumpmath.org**.) Our approach is designed to build equity by supporting the full spectrum of learners to achieve success in math.

Confidence Building is Key

JUMP Math begins each grade with review to enable every student to quickly develop the confidence needed to engage deeply with math. Our distinctive incremental approach to learning math concepts gradually increases the level of difficulty for students, empowering them to become motivated, independent problem solvers. Our books are also designed with simple pictures and models to avoid overwhelming learners when introducing new concepts, enabling them to see the deep structure of the math and gain the confidence to solve a wide range of math problems.

About JUMP Math

JUMP Math is a non-profit organization dedicated to helping every child in every classroom develop confidence, understanding, and a love of math. JUMP Math also offers a comprehensive set of classroom resources for students in Kindergarten to Grade 8.

For more information, visit JUMP Math at: www.jumpmath.org.

Contents

1. Arshalls Arrays

When you multiply two numbers, the result is called the **product** of the numbers.
In the **array** below, there are 3 **rows** of dots. There are 5 dots **in each row**.

5
10
15

Carmelle counts the dots by skip counting by 5s.

Carmelle writes a multiplication equation for the array: **3 × 5 = 15** (3 rows of 5 dots is 15 dots).

1. How many rows are there? How many dots in each row?
Write a multiplication equation for each array.

a)

___3___ rows

___4___ dots in each row

___3 × 4 = 12___

b)

_____ rows

_____ dots in each row

_____

c)

_____ rows

_____ dots in each row

_____

2. Write a product for each array.

a)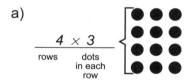

___4 × 3___
rows   dots
in each
row

b)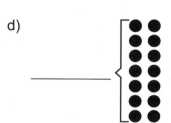

_____

c)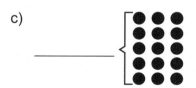

_____

d)

_____

3. Draw arrays for these products.

a) 5 × 5   b) 3 × 5   c) 2 × 4   d) 4 × 3   e) 1 × 6   f) 2 × 5

4. Draw an array and write a multiplication equation to find each answer.

a) On a bus, 4 people can sit in a row. There are 6 rows of seats on the bus. How many people can ride on the bus?

b) In a garden, there are 3 rows of plants. There are 5 plants in each row. How many plants are there altogether?

c) Jenny planted 8 seeds in each row. There are 4 rows of seeds. How many seeds did Jenny plant?

We can group the dots in this array: by rows: or by columns:

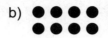

$3 \times 4 = 12$

$4 \times 3 = 12$

5. Group the dots by rows then by columns. Write two multiplication equations.

a) ●●●●● ●●●●●
   ●●●●● ●●●●●

   _____   _____

b) ●●●● ●●●●
   ●●●● ●●●●

   _____   _____

c)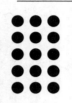

   _____   _____

d) ●●●●● ●●●●●
   ●●●●● ●●●●●
   ●●●●● ●●●●●
   ●●●●● ●●●●●

   _____   _____

6. Fill in the blanks.

a) 2 rows of 5 dots each is the same as _____ columns of _____ dots each, so $2 \times 5 =$ _____ $\times$ _____ .

b) 3 rows of 7 dots each is the same as _____ columns of _____ dots each, so $3 \times 7 =$ _____ $\times$ _____ .

c) 5 rows of 8 dots each is the same as _____ .

   _____ so $5 \times 8 =$ _____ .

7. a) The picture shows _____ rows of _____ dots each.

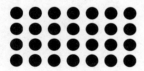

b) Now turn the page sideways.

   After turning the page sideways, the picture shows _____ rows of _____ dots each.

c) Did turning the page change the number of dots in the picture? _____

d) Write an equation that shows your answer to c). _____ $\times$ _____ = _____ $\times$ _____

8. Draw a picture to show that $2 \times 7 = 7 \times 2$.

2. Multiplication and Addition

Multiplying is a short way of adding: $4 \times 5 = \underbrace{5 + 5 + 5 + 5}$

add 5 four times

1. Write a sum for each product.

   a) $3 \times 4 = 4 + 4 + 4$ b) $2 \times 8 =$ c) $5 \times 6 =$

   d) $4 \times 2 =$ e) $3 \times 5 =$ f) $6 \times 3 =$

   g) $5 \times 7 =$ h) $2 \times 1 =$ i) $1 \times 8 =$

2. Write a product for each sum.

   a) $4 + 4 + 4 = 3 \times 4$ b) $5 + 5 + 5 =$ c) $4 + 4 =$

   d) $2 + 2 + 2 =$ e) $9 + 9 + 9 + 9 =$ f) $1 + 1 + 1 =$

   g) $6 + 6 + 6 + 6 + 6 =$ h) $8 + 8 + 8 + 8 + 8 =$ i) $3 + 3 + 3 + 3 =$

3. Write a sum and a product for each picture.

   a) 3 boxes; 2 pencils in each box

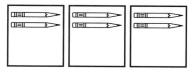

   —————— $2 + 2 + 2$ ——————

   —————— 3×2 ——————

   b) 3 boxes; 4 pencils in each box

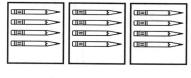

   ————————————————

   ————————————————

   c) 4 boxes; 3 pencils in each box

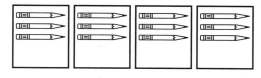

   ————————————————

   ————————————————

   d) 2 boxes; 5 pencils in each box

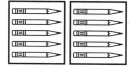

   ————————————————

   ————————————————

   e) 5 boxes; 3 pencils in each box

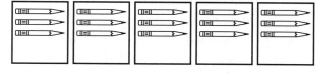

   ————————————————

   ————————————————

   f) 4 boxes; 2 pencils in each box

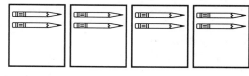

   ————————————————

   ————————————————

4. Add the numbers. Write your subtotals in the boxes provided.

        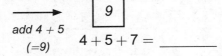   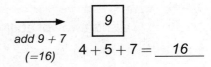

Example: $4 + 5 + 7 =$ _____   *add 4 + 5* (=9) $4 + 5 + 7 =$ _____   *add 9 + 7* (=16) $4 + 5 + 7 =$ ___16___

a) $2 + 3 + 5 =$ _____   b) $3 + 3 + 7 =$ _____   c) $5 + 4 + 3 =$ _____

d) $6 + 4 + 2 =$ _____   e) $8 + 3 + 4 =$ _____   f) $9 + 1 + 6 =$ _____

g) $4 + 3 + 3 + 2 =$ _____   h) $4 + 5 + 5 + 3 =$ _____   i) $6 + 7 + 3 + 5 =$ _____

5. Write a sum for each picture. Add to find out how many apples there are altogether.
Check your answer by counting the apples.

a) 3 boxes; 3 apples in each box

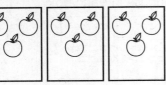

b) 4 boxes; 2 apples in each box

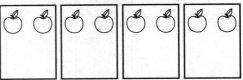

c) 4 boxes; 4 apples in each box

d) 3 boxes; 5 apples in each box

6. Draw a picture, and write a sum and a product for your picture.

a) 3 vans
7 people in each van

b) 4 bags
5 books in each bag

c) 6 boxes
4 pens in each box

d) 5 boats
4 kids in each boat

7. Write a sum and a product for each situation.

a) 6 plates
8 cookies on each plate

b) 7 bags
3 gifts in each bag

c) 4 baskets
7 bananas in each basket

3. Multiplying by Skip Counting

Zainab finds the **product of 3 and 5** by skip counting on a number line.

She counts off three 5s:

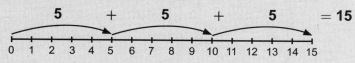

From the picture, Zainab can see that the product of 3 and 5 is 15: **3 × 5 = 15**.

1. Show how to find the products by skip counting.
    Use arrows like the ones in Zainab's picture.

    a) 4 × 3 =

    b) 7 × 2 =

2. Use the number line to skip count by 4s, 6s, and 7s. Fill in the boxes as you count.

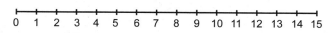

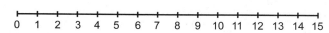

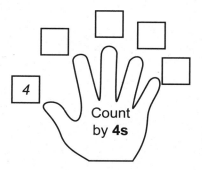

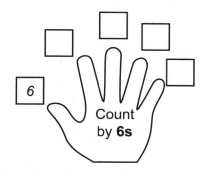

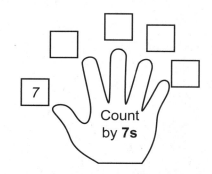

3. Find the products by skip counting on your fingers. Use the hands from Question 2 to help.

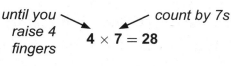

    a) 4 × 5 =   b) 5 × 2 =   c) 4 × 4 =   d) 2 × 6 =   e) 7 × 1 =

    f) 3 × 7 =   g) 3 × 3 =   h) 6 × 1 =   i) 2 × 7 =   j) 5 × 5 =

4. Find the number of items by skip counting. Write a multiplication equation
    for each picture.

    a)

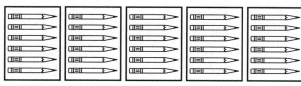
    b)

_____

_____

4. Times as Many

1. Draw 3 times as many circles as there are squares.

a) 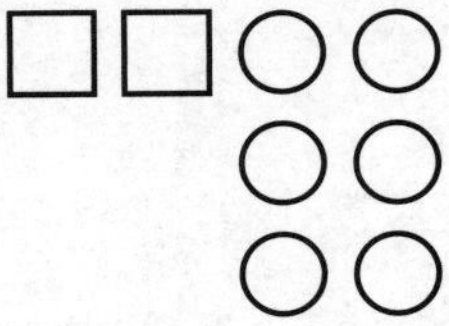 □ □ ○ ○
   ○ ○
   ○ ○

b) □

c) □ □ □

2. Write how many times as many circles as squares.

a) 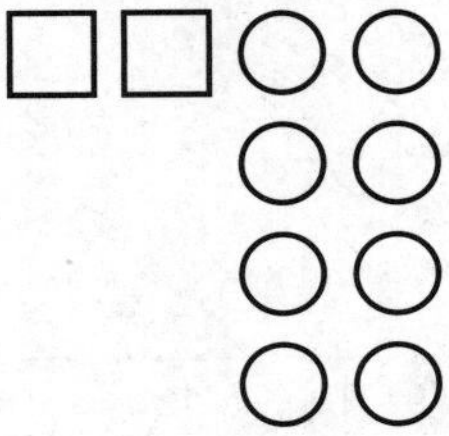 □ □ ○ ○
   ○ ○
   ○ ○
   ○ ○

There are _____ times as many circles as squares.

b) 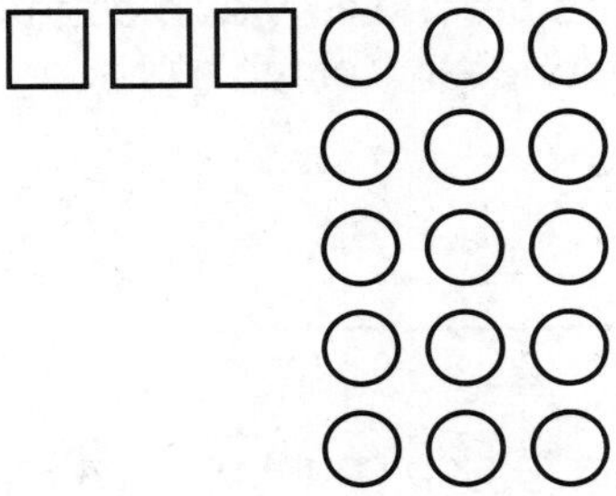 □ □ □ ○ ○ ○
   ○ ○ ○
   ○ ○ ○
   ○ ○ ○
   ○ ○ ○

There are _____ times as many circles as squares.

c) 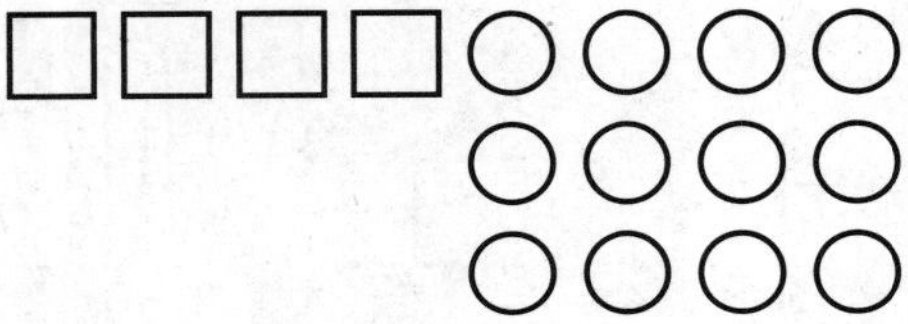 □ □ □ □ ○ ○ ○ ○
   ○ ○ ○ ○
   ○ ○ ○ ○

There are _____ times as many circles as squares.

d) 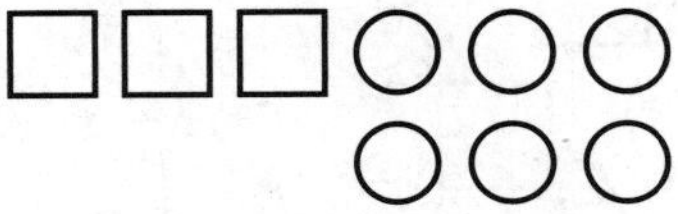 □ □ □ ○ ○ ○
   ○ ○ ○

There are _____ times as many circles as squares.

3. Draw a picture and then fill in the blanks.

a) Draw twice as many circles as squares.

□ □ □

b) Draw 4 times as many circles as squares.

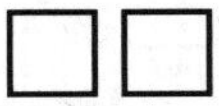

□ □

_____ × _____ = _____
number of   number of
squares   of circles

_____ × _____ = _____
number of   number of
squares   circles

There are 2 squares and 6 circles.

There are 3 times as many circles as squares.

We can say "6 is 3 times as many as 2."

$$3 \times 2 = 6$$

4. a) Kyle

Rema

b) Sam

Ravi

Rema has _____ times as many stickers as Kyle

_____ is _____ times as many as _____.

Ravi has _____ times as many stickers as Sam.

_____ is _____ times as many as _____.

5. The magnifying glass makes each object look twice as big.

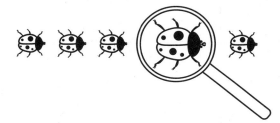

Actual length of object	Length under the magnifying glass
2 cm	
5 cm	
7 cm	

6. Use the multiplication equation to write how many times as many one number is than the other.

a) $35 = 5 \times 7$

35 is _____ times as many as 7

b) $40 = 5 \times 8$

40 is _____ times as many as 8

c) $30 = 10 \times 3$

30 is _____ times as many as 3

d) $42 = 6 \times 7$

42 is _____ times as many as 7

7. Draw a picture and write a multiplication equation.

a) There are 2 circles. There are 4 times as many triangles as circles.

b) There are 2 boys. There are 3 times as many girls as boys.

c) There are 4 blue marbles. There are twice as many red marbles as blue marbles.

8. Kyle has 6 books. Ron has three times as many books.
How many books does Ron have? Explain how you know.

5. Place Value—Ones, Tens, Hundreds, and Thousands

1. Write the place value of the underlined digit.

   a) 3,5<u>6</u>4   *tens*   b) 1,<u>3</u>36

   c) 25<u>6</u>   d) <u>1</u>,230

   e) <u>3</u>,859   f) 5,<u>7</u>45   g) 2<u>3</u>8

   h) 6,<u>2</u>14   i) 8<u>7</u>   j) <u>9</u>,430

2. Write the place value of the digit 5 in each of the numbers below.
   Hint: First underline the 5 in each number.

   a) 5,640   b) 547   c) 451

   d) 2,415   e) 1,257   f) 5,643

   g) 1,563   h) 56   i) 205

You can also write numbers using a place value chart. Example:

This is the number 3,264 in a place value chart:

Thousands	Hundreds	Tens	Ones
3	2	6	4

3. Write the following numbers into the place value chart.

		Thousands	Hundreds	Tens	Ones
a)	5,231	5	2	3	1
b)	8,053				
c)	489				
d)	27				
e)	9,104				
f)	4,687				
g)	7,060				
h)	760				

6. Representation with Base Ten Materials

1. Write each number in expanded form
(numerals and words), then as a numeral.

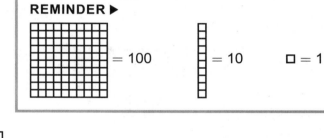
Example:

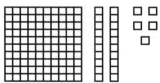

___1___ hundred + ___2___ tens + ___5___ ones = | 125 |

a)

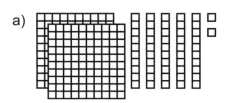

____ hundreds + ____ tens + ____ ones = | |

b)

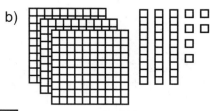

____ hundreds + ____ tens + ____ ones = | |

c)

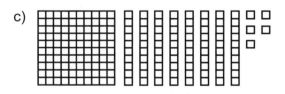

____ hundred + ____ tens + ____ ones = | |

d)

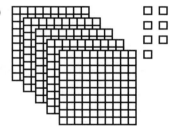

____ hundreds + ____ tens + ____ ones = | |

2. Draw the base ten model for the number.

Example: 123

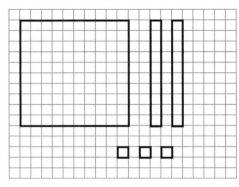

132

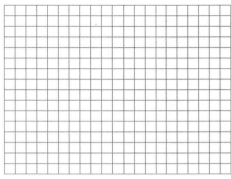

3. Draw the base ten model for the number.

a) 68   b) 350   c) 249

4. Write each number in expanded form
(numerals and words), then as a numeral.

Example:

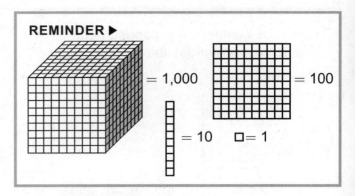

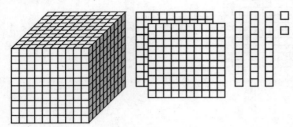

__1__ thousand + __2__ hundreds + __3__ tens + __2__ ones = | *1,232* |

a)

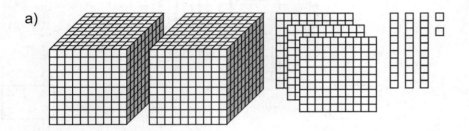

____ thousands + ____ hundreds + ____ tens + ____ ones = | |

b)

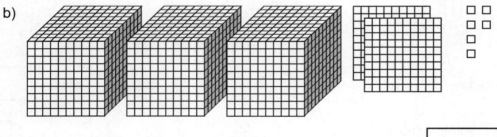

____ thousands + ____ hundreds + ____ tens + ____ ones = | |

c)

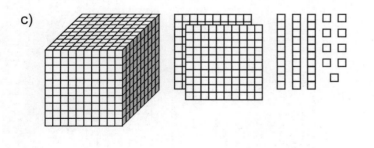

_____

7. Adding with Regrouping

1. Add the numbers by drawing a picture and by adding the digits.
   Use base ten materials to show how to combine the numbers and how to regroup.

a) $16 + 25$

	With base ten materials		With numerals	
	Tens	**Ones**	**Tens**	**Ones**
16	▯	□ □ □ □ □ □	1	6
25	▯ ▯	□ □ □ □ □	2	5
sum	▯ ▯ ▯	⟨□ □ □ □ □⟩ □ *10 ones = 1 ten*	3	11
	▯ ▯ ▯ ▯	□	4	1

$16 + 25 = \underline{\quad 41 \quad}$

b) $25 + 37$

	With base ten materials		With numerals	
	Tens	**Ones**	**Tens**	**Ones**
25				
37				
sum				

$25 + 37 = \underline{\qquad}$

c) $29 + 36$

	With base ten materials		With numerals	
	Tens	**Ones**	**Tens**	**Ones**
29				
36				
sum				

$29 + 36 = \underline{\qquad}$

d) $18 + 35$

	With base ten materials		With numerals	
	Tens	**Ones**	**Tens**	**Ones**
18				
35				
sum				

$18 + 35 = \underline{\qquad}$

2. Add the numbers by regrouping.

Step 1: Regroup 10 ones as 1 ten.

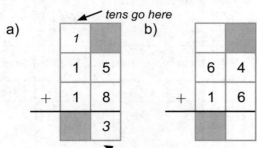

tens go here

a)

	1
1	5
+ 1	8
	3

ones go here

b)

6	4
+ 1	6

c)

7	5
+ 1	9

d)

6	6
+ 1	7

e)

1	5
+ 3	8

f)

1	3
+ 1	9

g)

2	4
+ 3	8

h)

5	4
+ 1	8

i)

2	7
+ 6	9

j)

4	6
+ 4	8

Step 2: Add the numbers in the tens column.

k)

1	
1	2
+ 1	8
3	0

l)

1	
1	3
+ 1	7
	0

m)

1	
1	5
+ 2	8
	3

n)

1	
2	6
+ 2	6
	2

o)

1	
3	8
+ 2	7
	5

3. Add the numbers by regrouping.

a)

1	
3	6
+ 1	8
5	4

b)

3	7
+ 1	8

c)

5	9
+ 1	8

d)

3	7
+ 4	3

e)

5	7
+ 2	6

f)

6	3
+ 2	9

g)

5	8
+ 4	7

h)

1	8
+ 7	7

i)

5	9
+ 1	3

j)

7	5
+ 1	6

Sometimes the sum of two 2-digit numbers is a 3-digit number.

Example:

	1		
		7	5
	+	8	2
	1	5	7

7 tens + 8 tens = 15 tens = 1 hundred + 5 tens, so we need to regroup 10 tens as 1 hundred.

4. Add by regrouping 10 tens as 1 hundred.

a)
	1		
		7	5
	+	8	2
	1	5	7

b)
		8	4
	+	6	3

c)
		7	2
	+	6	5

d)
		9	1
	+	9	6

e)
		8	5
	+	7	3

5. Add by regrouping 10 ones as 1 ten and 10 tens as 1 hundred.

a)
	1	1	
		7	5
	+	6	7
	1	4	2

b)
		8	6
	+	3	9

c)
		5	8
	+	4	7

d)
		7	6
	+	7	8

e)
		3	5
	+	6	5

```
      1
      8  6
  +   7  9
  ─────────
  1   6  5
```

You need to regroup 6 + 9 = 15 as 1 ten and 5 ones, but you can write 1 + 8 + 7 tens = 16 tens directly.

6. Add by regrouping when you need to.

a)
	8	5
+	3	4

b)
	7	4
+	2	8

c)
	7	9
+	8	8

d)
	6	4
+	3	9

e)
	7	5
+	2	5

7. Add by regrouping. Use grid paper.

a) 37 + 48   b) 29 + 83   c) 66 + 39   d) 75 + 48   e) 91 + 87

8. Adding 3-Digit Numbers

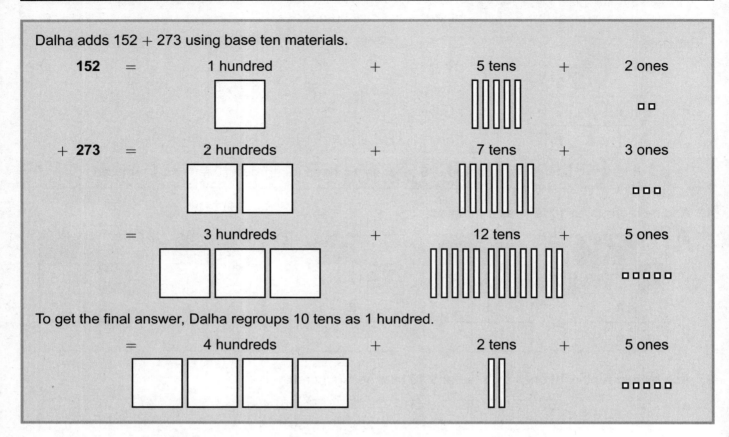

Dalha adds 152 + 273 using base ten materials.

| 152 | = | 1 hundred | + | 5 tens | + | 2 ones |

| + 273 | = | 2 hundreds | + | 7 tens | + | 3 ones |

| | = | 3 hundreds | + | 12 tens | + | 5 ones |

To get the final answer, Dalha regroups 10 tens as 1 hundred.

| | = | 4 hundreds | + | 2 tens | + | 5 ones |

1. Add the numbers using base ten materials or a picture. Record your work below.

a)   353

    + 164

_____ hundreds + _____ tens + _____ ones

+ _____ hundred + _____ tens + _____ ones

= _____ hundreds + _____ tens + _____ ones

after regrouping

= _____ hundreds + _____ ten + _____ ones

b)   462

    + 375

_____ hundreds + _____ tens + _____ ones

+ _____ hundreds + _____ tens + _____ ones

= _____ hundreds + _____ tens + _____ ones

after regrouping

= _____ hundreds + _____ tens + _____ ones

2. Add. You will need to regroup.

a)
```
  1
  5 2 6
+ 2 9 3
  8 1 9
```

b)
```
  ⬚
  6 4 5
+ 1 8 3
```

c)
```
  ⬚
  3 7 4
+ 4 6 2
```

d)
```
  4 8 2
+ 4 7 7
```

e)
```
  2 8 4
+ 5 9 5
```

3. Add, regrouping where necessary.

a)
```
    3  2  8
+      1  4
```

b)
```
    7  4  7
+   5  1  6
```

c)
```
    9  1  5
+      4  5
```

d)
```
    3  4  6
+   2  0  5
```

e)
```
    2  1  8
+   3  4  8
```

f)
```
    5  6  4
+   5  5  3
```

g)
```
    7  4  8
+   4  2  4
```

h)
```
    7  2  6
+   6  4  8
```

i)
```
    5  6  4
+   6  7  2
```

j)
```
    4  4  4
+   2  0  9
```

4. Line the numbers up correctly in the grid, then add.

a) 218 + 265   b) 272 + 213   c) 643 + 718   d) 937 + 25

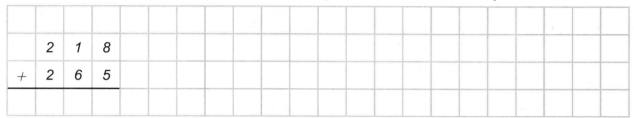

e) 146 + 273   f) 816 + 925   g) 369 + 119   h) 847 + 910

5. Add. You will need to regroup twice.

a)
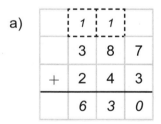
```
   1  1
   3  8  7
+  2  4  3
   6  3  0
```

b)
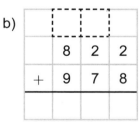
```
   8  2  2
+  9  7  8
```

c)
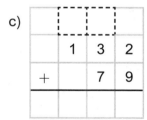
```
   1  3  2
+     7  9
```

d)
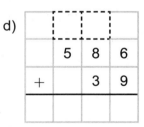
```
   5  8  6
+     3  9
```

BONUS ▶

Use the pattern in your answers to a), b), and c) to find the sums in d) and e) without adding.

a)
```
    9
+   9
```

b)
```
   9  9
+  9  9
```

c)
```
   9  9  9
+  9  9  9
```

d)
```
   9, 9  9  9
+  9, 9  9  9
```

e)
```
   9  9, 9  9  9
+  9  9, 9  9  9
```

6. Add the numbers. Use grid paper.

a) 22 + 36 + 21   b) 324 + 112 + 422   c) 248 + 167 + 539

9. Adding Larger Numbers

Amber adds 1,852 + 2,321 using base ten materials.

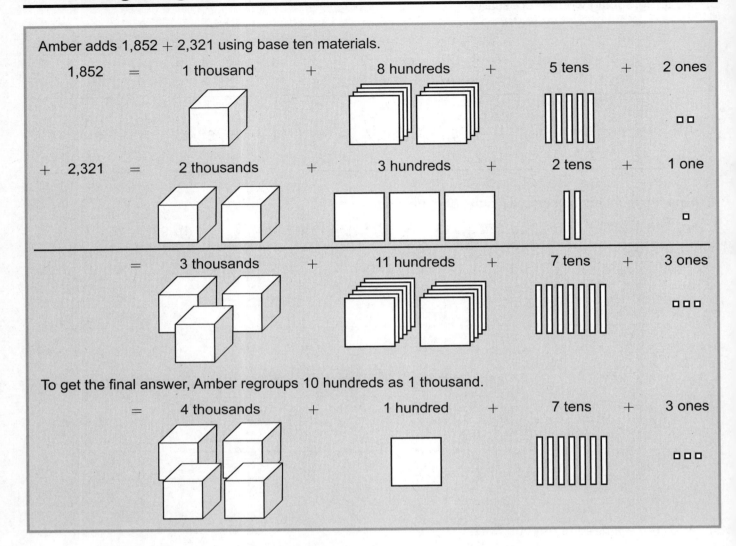

1,852	=	1 thousand	+	8 hundreds	+	5 tens	+	2 ones
+ 2,321	=	2 thousands	+	3 hundreds	+	2 tens	+	1 one
	=	3 thousands	+	11 hundreds	+	7 tens	+	3 ones

To get the final answer, Amber regroups 10 hundreds as 1 thousand.

	=	4 thousands	+	1 hundred	+	7 tens	+	3 ones

1. Add the numbers and record your work below. Use base ten materials or draw a picture to show the addition.

a) 2,543   _____ thousands + _____ hundreds + _____ tens + _____ ones

    + 3,621   + _____ thousands + _____ hundreds + _____ tens + _____ one

                = _____ thousands + _____ hundreds + _____ tens + _____ ones

   after regrouping   = _____ thousands + _____ hundred + _____ tens + _____ ones

b) 3,824   _____ thousands + _____ hundreds + _____ tens + _____ ones

    + 1,654   + _____ thousand + _____ hundreds + _____ tens + _____ ones

                = _____ thousands + _____ hundreds + _____ tens + _____ ones

   after regrouping   = _____ thousands + _____ hundreds + _____ tens + _____ ones

2. Add. (You will need to regroup.)

a)
```
    1
  5,2 6 5
+ 2,9 1 2
─────────
  8,1 7 7
```

b)
```
  6,4 5 4
+ 1,8 3 3
─────────
```

c)
```
  3,7 4 7
+ 2,6 2 1
─────────
```

d)
```
  1,8 2 1
+ 2,7 7 2
─────────
```

e)
```
  1,8 2 4
+ 5,7 7 3
─────────
```

3. Add. You will need to regroup 10 tens as 1 hundred.

a)
```
  3,4 8 3
+ 1,3 3 4
─────────
```

b)
```
  2,5 6 9
+ 1,2 6 0
─────────
```

c)
```
  5,4 8 6
+ 1,1 3 1
─────────
```

d)
```
  8,3 6 4
+ 1,4 7 2
─────────
```

e)
```
  1,2 9 4
+ 5,0 9 3
─────────
```

4. Add. You will need to regroup 10 ones as 1 ten.

a)
```
  2,4 3 6
+ 1,1 2 5
─────────
```

b)
```
  8,1 2 7
+ 1,7 4 3
─────────
```

c)
```
  7,5 8 8
+ 2,1 0 8
─────────
```

d)
```
  5,4 2 5
+ 2,3 4 7
─────────
```

e)
```
  6,2 5 4
+ 2,6 3 9
─────────
```

5. Add by regrouping where necessary.

a)
```
  2,3 5 4
+ 2,8 3 1
─────────
```

b)
```
  9,6 8 3
+ 1,7 4 2
─────────
```

c)
```
  5,8 7 1
+ 4,8 3 3
─────────
```

d)
```
  8,5 2 5
+ 1,5 3 3
─────────
```

e)
```
  9,8 7 9
+ 2,7 2 3
─────────
```

f)
```
  7,5 4 6
+ 4,8 2 2
─────────
```

g)
```
  7,6 2 4
+ 1,6 0 1
─────────
```

h)
```
  6,6 9 0
+ 3,7 1 2
─────────
```

i)
```
  9,9 7 5
+ 3,7 5 1
─────────
```

j)
```
  3,9 4 5
+ 3,4 5 1
─────────
```

k)
```
  4,5 3 4
+ 2,5 4 2
─────────
```

l)
```
  6,7 5 4
+ 1,3 6 0
─────────
```

m)
```
  3,2 1 4
+ 4,8 5 2
─────────
```

n)
```
  2,5 0 9
+   6 2 1
─────────
```

o)
```
  5,3 7 2
+   5 2 1
─────────
```

p)
```
  6,8 2 7
+     8 5
─────────
```

q)
```
  9,8 5 6
+   7 4 2
─────────
```

r)
```
  4,3 2 1
+ 5,9 3 2
─────────
```

s)
```
  6,2 3 1
+ 7,4 8 9
─────────
```

t)
```
  8,0 3 2
+   5 1 8
─────────
```

6. Add, regrouping where necessary.

a)
```
  3 5,8 4 6
+ 2 1,1 3 5
```

b)
```
  4 3,5 6 4
+ 8 2,8 1 3
```

c)
```
  5 6,5 3 4
+    3,2 9 4
```

d)
```
  9 8,8 5 4
+    1,0 6 3
```

e)
```
  2 5 6,7 5 2
+ 3 7 2,3 3 4
```

f)
```
  6 9 3,4 7 3
+ 8 5 5,2 4 3
```

g)
```
  3 5 6,7 5 3
+      9,2 3 3
```

h)
```
  4 7 8,2 3 0
+      3,4 8 8
```

7. Add by lining the digits up correctly in the grid. In some questions you may have to regroup twice.

a) 2,468 + 7,431   b) 8,596 + 1,235   c) 6,650 + 2,198   d) 8,359 + 48

 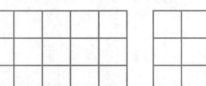  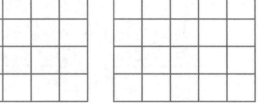

e) 73,246 + 18,382   f) 145,683 + 329,234

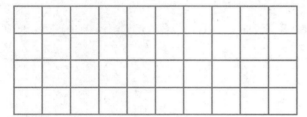 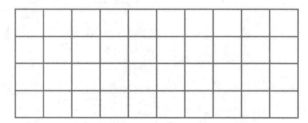

8. Add, regrouping where necessary.

a) 5,326 + 1,234 + 6,762   b) 3,658 + 6,343 + 4,534   c) 389 + 3,247 + 712 + 52

BONUS ▶

A **palindrome** is a number (or word) that reads the same forward and backward.

For example: 363, 51,815 and 2,375,732 are all palindromes.

You can create a palindrome from any number. Example:

Step 1: Start with 124. Reverse the digits.   124 → 421

Step 2: Add the two numbers.   124 + 421 = 545

Step 3: If the sum in Step 2 is not a palindrome, repeat Steps 1 and 2
with the new number. Most numbers will eventually become
palindromes if you keep repeating these steps.

Create palindromes from the following numbers.

a) 216   b) 154   c) 651   d) 23,153   e) 371   f) 258   g) 1,385

10. Subtraction

To subtract 48 − 32, Bradley makes a model of 48.

Then he crosses out 3 tens and 2 ones because 32 = 3 tens + 2 ones.

48   48 − 32   =   16

1. Subtract by crossing out tens and ones blocks. Draw your final answer in the right-hand box.

a)

39 − 18	= 21
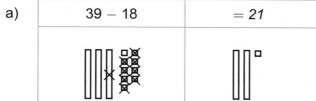	

b)

25 − 11	=

c)

43 − 21	=

d)

45 − 32	=

2. Write how many tens and ones in each number. Then subtract the tens and ones to find the final answer.

a)   45 = _4_ tens + _5_ ones
    − 32 = _3_ tens + _2_ ones
       = _1_ ten + _3_ ones
       = _13_

b)   57 = ___ tens + ___ ones
    − 34 = ___ tens + ___ ones
       = ___ tens + ___ ones
       = _____

c)   84 = ___ tens + ___ ones
    − 63 = ___ tens + ___ ones
       = ___ tens + ___ one
       = _____

d)   89 = ___ tens + ___ ones
    − 56 = ___ tens + ___ ones
       = ___ tens + ___ ones
       = _____

e)   77 = ___ tens + ___ ones
    − 44 = ___ tens + ___ ones
       = ___ tens + ___ ones
       = _____

f)   67 = ___ tens + ___ ones
    − 45 = ___ tens + ___ ones
       = ___ tens + ___ ones
       = _____

3. Subtract by writing the number of tens and ones in each number.

a)
$$36 = 30 + 6$$
$$-\ 24 = 20 + 4$$
$$= 10 + 2$$
$$= 12$$

b)
$$84 =$$
$$-\ 52 =$$
$$=$$
$$=$$

c)
$$98 =$$
$$-\ 37 =$$
$$=$$
$$=$$

d)
$$73 =$$
$$-\ 12 =$$

e)
$$26 =$$
$$-\ 24 =$$

f)
$$88 =$$
$$-\ 33 =$$

4. Subtract the numbers by subtracting the digits.

a)
```
  5 4
- 2 3
```

b)
```
  8 6
- 7 3
```

c)
```
  3 6
- 1 5
```

d)
```
  6 4
- 3 2
```

e)
```
  9 5
- 4 2
```

f)
```
  8 9
- 4 0
```

5. a) Draw a picture of 543 using hundreds, tens, and ones blocks.
   Show how you would subtract 543 − 421.

   b) Now subtract 543 − 421 by lining up the digits and subtracting. Do you get the same answer?

6. Subtract.

a)
```
  7, 5 3 2
- 4, 1 2 1
```

b)
```
  6 5, 3 5 6
- 4 4, 2 4 5
```

c)
```
  9 5 5, 7 6 3
- 5 2 3, 0 1 1
```

11. Subtraction with Regrouping

Farkan subtracts 46 − 18 using base ten materials.

Step 1:
Farkan represents 46 with base ten materials.

Tens	Ones
4	6

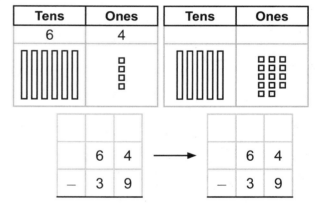

Here is how Farkan uses numerals to show his work:

$$\begin{array}{r} 46 \\ -\,18 \\ \hline \end{array}$$

Step 2:
8 (the ones digit of 18) is greater than 6 (the ones digit of 46) so Farkan regroups 1 tens block as 10 ones blocks.

Tens	Ones
3	16

Here is how Farkan shows the regrouping:

$$\begin{array}{r} \overset{3}{\cancel{4}}\overset{16}{\cancel{6}} \\ -\,1\,8 \\ \hline \end{array}$$

Step 3:
Farkan subtracts 18 (he takes away 1 tens block and 8 ones blocks).

Tens	Ones
2	8

And now Farkan can subtract 16 − 8 ones and 3 − 1 tens:

$$\begin{array}{r} \overset{3}{\cancel{4}}\overset{16}{\cancel{6}} \\ -\,1\,8 \\ \hline 2\,8 \end{array}$$

1. In these questions, Farkan doesn't have enough ones to subtract. Help him by regrouping 1 tens block as 10 ones. Show how he would change his subtraction statement.

a) **63 − 26**

Tens	Ones
6	3

Tens	Ones
5	13

	Tens	Ones
	6	3
−	2	6

⟶

	Tens	Ones
	5	13
	$\cancel{6}$	$\cancel{3}$
−	2	6

b) **64 − 39**

Tens	Ones
6	4

Tens	Ones

	Tens	Ones
	6	4
−	3	9

⟶

	Tens	Ones
	6	4
−	3	9

c) **42 − 19**

Tens	Ones
4	2

Tens	Ones

	Tens	Ones
	4	2
−	1	9

⟶

	Tens	Ones
	4	2
−	1	9

d) **35 − 27**

Tens	Ones
3	5

Tens	Ones

	Tens	Ones
	3	5
−	2	7

⟶

	Tens	Ones
	3	5
−	2	7

2. Subtract by regrouping.

a)
	3	13
	$\cancel{4}$	$\cancel{3}$
−	2	7
	1	6

b)
	5	6
−	1	8

c)
	6	4
−	3	9

d)
	7	0
−	2	8

e)
	5	5
−	3	7

f)
	8	0
−	5	7

g)
	3	8
−	1	9

h)
	2	2
−		6

i)
	4	4
−		9

j)
	9	0
−	7	5

3. For the questions where you need to regroup, write "regroup" in the blank.
If you don't need to regroup, write "OK." Then find the answer.

a)
$$\begin{array}{r} {\scriptstyle 4\ 14} \\ \cancel{5}\cancel{4} \\ -\ 19 \\ \hline 35 \end{array}$$ regroup
4 is less than 9

b)
$$\begin{array}{r} 77 \\ -\ 56 \\ \hline \end{array}$$ OK

c)
$$\begin{array}{r} 85 \\ -\ 53 \\ \hline \end{array}$$ _____

d)
$$\begin{array}{r} 95 \\ -\ 18 \\ \hline \end{array}$$ _____

e)
$$\begin{array}{r} 66 \\ -\ 54 \\ \hline \end{array}$$ _____

f)
$$\begin{array}{r} 84 \\ -\ 17 \\ \hline \end{array}$$ _____

g)
$$\begin{array}{r} 82 \\ -\ 29 \\ \hline \end{array}$$ _____

h)
$$\begin{array}{r} 26 \\ -\ 15 \\ \hline \end{array}$$ _____

i)
$$\begin{array}{r} 45 \\ -\ 9 \\ \hline \end{array}$$ _____

j)
$$\begin{array}{r} 12 \\ -\ 8 \\ \hline \end{array}$$ _____

k)
$$\begin{array}{r} 30 \\ -\ 19 \\ \hline \end{array}$$ _____

l)
$$\begin{array}{r} 52 \\ -\ 9 \\ \hline \end{array}$$ _____

m)
$$\begin{array}{r} 47 \\ -\ 19 \\ \hline \end{array}$$ _____

n)
$$\begin{array}{r} 23 \\ -\ 8 \\ \hline \end{array}$$ _____

o)
$$\begin{array}{r} 60 \\ -\ 49 \\ \hline \end{array}$$ _____

p)
$$\begin{array}{r} 80 \\ -\ 41 \\ \hline \end{array}$$ _____

q)
$$\begin{array}{r} 93 \\ -\ 24 \\ \hline \end{array}$$ _____

r)
$$\begin{array}{r} 79 \\ -\ 42 \\ \hline \end{array}$$ _____

4. Subtract by regrouping 1 hundred as 10 tens. The first one has been started for you.

a)

	2	11	
	~~3~~	~~7~~	5
−	1	6	2

b)

	5	3	8
−	2	9	5

c)

	3	1	7
−	1	8	6

d)

	9	4	2
−	5	7	0

5. For the questions below, you will have to regroup *twice*. Example:

Step 1
```
      4 14
    8 5̷ 4̷
  − 3 6 7
```

Step 2
```
      4 14
    8 5̷ 4̷
  − 3 6 7
          7
```

Step 3
```
         14
    7 5̷ 14
    8̷ 5̷ 4̷
  − 3 6 7
          7
```

Step 4
```
         14
    7 5̷ 14
    8̷ 5̷ 4̷
  − 3 6 7
        8 7
```

Step 5
```
         14
    7 5̷ 14
    8̷ 5̷ 4̷
  − 3 6 7
      4 8 7
```

a)

	6	3	4
−	1	5	6

b)

	5	8	5
−		9	6

c)

	5	3	2
−	2	3	5

d)

	8	5	4
−	3	7	7

To subtract 3,245 − 1,923, Sara regroups 1 thousands block as 10 hundreds blocks.

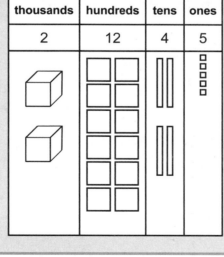

thousands	hundreds	tens	ones
3	2	4	5

thousands	hundreds	tens	ones
2	12	4	5

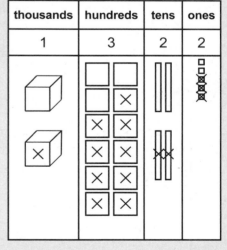

thousands	hundreds	tens	ones
1	3	2	2

6. Subtract by regrouping 1 thousand as 10 hundreds.

a)

	7	13		
	~~8~~	~~3~~	6	4
−	4	8	3	1
	3	*5*	*3*	*3*

b)

	5	6	9	3
−	2	7	1	1

c)

	5	7	5	8
−	2	9	4	2

12. Parts and Totals

1. The bars in each picture represent quantities of red and green apples. Fill in the blanks.

   a) 5 red apples
      3 green apples

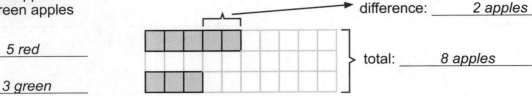

      <u>5 red</u>   difference: ___<u>2 apples</u>___

      <u>3 green</u>   total: ___<u>8 apples</u>___

   b) 4 green apples
      2 more red apples than green apples

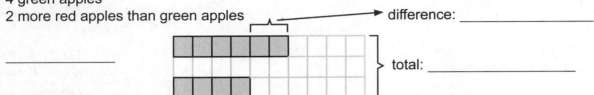

      _____   difference: _____

      _____   total: _____

   c) 7 green apples
      3 more green apples than red apple

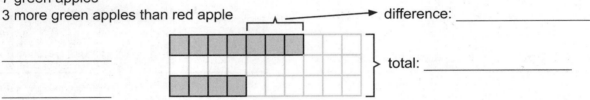

      _____   difference: _____

      _____   total: _____

   d) 10 apples in total
      3 green apples

      _____   difference: _____

      _____   total: _____

2. Complete the table.

	Red Apples	Green Apples	Total Number of Apples	How many more of one color of apple?
a)	2	5	7	3 more green apples than red
b)	3		8	
c)		2	9	
d)	4			1 more red apple than green

3. Draw a picture (as in Question 1) and make a table (as in Question 2) for the quantities.

   a) 4 red apples
      4 more green apples
      than red apples

   b) 12 apples in total
      7 green apples

   BONUS ▶ 10 apples in total
           2 more red apples
           than green apples

		Parts 1 and 2
4 green marbles		
5 red marbles		
9 marbles altogether	**Total**	

4. Draw a picture on grid paper (as in Question 1) to complete each row.
Circle the number in the table that answers each question.

		Part 1	Part 2	Total	Difference Between Parts
a)	Helen has 7 green marbles and 9 red marbles. How many marbles does she have?	7	9	(16)	2
b)	Helen has 12 green marbles and 4 red marbles. How many more green marbles than red marbles does she have?				
c)	A sandwich costs 3 dollars, and a drink costs 1 dollar. How much do the sandwich and the drink cost together?				
d)	A sandwich costs 5 dollars, and a drink costs 2 dollars. How much less than a sandwich does the drink cost?				
e)	Peter biked 9 miles. Lavi biked 6 miles. How many miles did they bike altogether?				
f)	Bilal jogged 8 miles. Hong jogged 12 miles. How much farther did Hong jog than Bilal?				

5. For each part of Question 4, was the answer the total, a part, or the difference?

a) _____*total*_____   b) _____

c) _____   d) _____

e) _____   f) _____

6. Draw a picture on grid paper (as in Question 1) for each problem.

a) Ron has 13 red stickers and 6 blue stickers. How many stickers does he have?

b) Claire has 6 pets. Two are dogs and the rest are cats. How many cats does she have?

c) Peter walked 7 miles. Lavi walked 3 miles. How much farther did Peter walk?

13. Parts and Totals (Advanced)

1. Fill in the table. Then circle the number that is the answer to the question.

		Green Grapes	Purple Grapes	Total Number of Grapes	Difference Between Types of Grapes
a)	There are 8 green grapes. There are 5 more green grapes than purple grapes. How many purple grapes are there?	8	③	11	5 more green than purple
b)	There are 7 green grapes. There are 12 grapes altogether. How many purple grapes are there?				
c)	There are 16 green grapes and 49 purple grapes. How many grapes are there altogether?				
d)	There are 7 more green grapes than purple grapes. There are 5 purple grapes. How many grapes are there altogether?				
e)	There are 17 green grapes. There are 32 grapes altogether. How many more green grapes than purple grapes are there?				
f)	There are 26 green grapes. There are 9 fewer purple grapes than green grapes. How many grapes are there altogether?				
g)	There are 5 more green grapes than purple grapes. There are 7 green grapes. How many grapes are there altogether?				

2.
   a) There are 7 dogs at the shelter. There are 3 more cats than dogs at the shelter. How many cats and dogs are at the shelter?

   b) There are apples and pears on the table. There are 8 apples and 3 fewer pears. How many apples and pears are on the table?

   c) Darya invited 17 friends to a birthday party. Seven of them are boys. How many more girls than boys did Darya invite to the party?

14. Fact Families

1. Write in words what each **equation** says.

    a) $3 + 5 = 8$ Start with _____, add _____ more, end up with _____.

    b) $7 - 4 = 3$ Start with _____, take away _____, end up with _____.

    c) $8 - 2 = 6$ _____.

    d) $5 + 4 = 9$ _____.

Jane and Bob each find how many circles altogether.

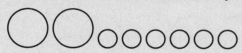

Jane starts with the big circles and writes $2 + 6 = 8$.

Bob starts with the small circles and writes $6 + 2 = 8$.

---

2. What does the first number represent?

    a)

    4 $+ 2 = 6$

    the small circles

    b)

    3 $+ 5 = 8$

    _____

    c)

    5 $+ 1 = 6$

    _____

    d)

    2 $+ 3 = 5$

    _____

3. Write two addition equations for each picture.

    a)

    Start with the big circles. _2 + 5 = 7_

    Start with the small circles. _5 + 2 = 7_

    b)

    Start with the big circles. _____

    Start with the small circles. _____

    c)

    Start with the big circles. _____

    Start with the small circles. _____

    d)

    Start with the big circles. _____

    Start with the small circles. _____

Jane and Bob each start with the same picture.

Jane takes away the big circles and writes $5 - 2 = 3$.

Bob takes away the small circles and writes $5 - 3 = 2$.

4. Write two subtraction equations for each picture.

a)

Take away the big circles. _____$7 - 3 = 4$_____

Take away the small circles. _____$7 - 4 = 3$_____

b)

Take away the big circles. _____

Take away the small circles. _____

c)

Take away the big circles. _____

Take away the small circles. _____

d)

Take away the big circles. _____

Take away the small circles. _____

You can write two addition equations and two subtraction equations for the picture.

$2 + 3 = 5$ $5 - 2 = 3$

$3 + 2 = 5$ $5 - 3 = 2$

The four equations make up a **fact family.**

---

5. Write the fact family for the picture.

a)

_____

_____

b)

_____

_____

6. Complete the fact family for each equation.

a) $3 + 6 = 9$

_____$6 + 3 = 9$_____

_____$9 - 6 = 3$_____

_____$9 - 3 = 6$_____

b) $8 - 1 = 7$

_____

_____

_____

c) $4 - 3 = 1$

_____

_____

_____

7. Write the fact family for $3 + 3 = 6$. How is it different from the fact families in Question 6?

8. Fill in the table.

	Green Grapes	Purple Grapes	Total Number of Grapes	Fact Family for Total	How many more of one type of grape?
a)	7	2	9	$7 + 2 = 9$ $2 + 7 = 9$ $9 - 2 = 7$ $9 - 7 = 2$	5 more green than purple
b)	6		10		
c)	2	9			
d)		5			4 more green than purple

9. Write the correct sign ($+$ or $-$) in the box.

a) number of green grapes ☐ number of purple grapes = how many more green than purple grapes

b) number of green grapes ☐ number of purple grapes = how many grapes altogether

c) number of grapes altogether ☐ number of green grapes = number of purple grapes

d) number of green grapes ☐ how many more purple than green grapes = how many purple grapes

e) number of purple grapes ☐ number of green grapes = how many more purple than green grapes

15. Sums and Differences

1. A glass can hold 255 kidney beans. How many beans can two glasses hold?

2. Alice's class raised $312 for charity. Sophie's class raised $287.

   a) Whose class raised more money? How did you find the answer?

   b) How much money did the two classes raise altogether?

3. At a summer camp, 324 children are enrolled in baseball. There are 128 *more* children enrolled in swimming than in baseball.

   a) How many children are enrolled in swimming?

   b) How many children are enrolled in swimming or baseball altogether?

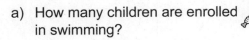

4. A coast redwood tree in California is 376 feet tall. The top of a treehouse in Crossville, Tennessee, is 97 feet above the ground.

How far above the top of the treehouse is the top of the tree?

5. Emma flies 2,457 miles on one day and 1,357 miles the next day.

How many miles did she fly in the two days?

6. What is the greatest 3-digit number you can add to 275 without having to regroup any place values?

275

7. The length of Falling Spring Cave in Missouri is 5,305 feet. The length of Fulford Cave in Colorado is 5,279 feet.

How much longer is Falling Spring Cave than Fulford Cave?

8. The border between the United States and Canada is about 5,525 miles long. The total length of the Great Wall of China, including its branches, is about 5,500 miles.

How much longer than the Great Wall of China is the Canada/US border?

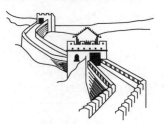

9. 2,375 tickets to a concert were sold one day, and 3,528 tickets were sold the next day.

How many tickets were sold altogether on those two days?

16. Larger Numbers (Review)

1. Write the place value of the underlined digit.

a) 1 2 ,6 4 3

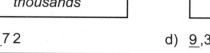

b) 2 3 ,1 2 1

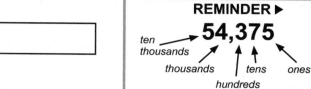
c) 6 0 ,1 7 2

d) 9 ,3 7 5

2. Write the numeral for the number words.

a) twenty-two thousand, five hundred forty-four

b) one thousand, four hundred twenty

c) sixty-three thousand, nine hundred thirty-six

d) five hundred four thousand, ninety

3. Write the number words for the numerals.

a) 61,145 = _____

b) 84,929 = _____

4. Write the number in expanded form (using numerals).

a) 17,359 = _____

b) 72,664 = _____

c) 50,137 = _____

5. Circle the greater number.

a) 142,727 or 25,848

b) 632,165 or 632,166

c) 498,400 or 497,500

6. Add or subtract.

a)
```
    1  4  2  6  3
 +  7  2  3  3  4
 _____
```

b)
```
    7  7  6  5  1
 +  1  2  3  4  8
 _____
```

c)
```
    8  1  6  4  2
 +     9  3  2  1
 _____
```

d)
```
    7  2  3  4  7
 -  3  1  1  1  2
 _____
```

e)
```
    5  7  8  3  6
 -  1  7  4  1  2
 _____
```

f)
```
    1  0  0  0  0
 -     7  1  6  2
 _____
```

17. Concepts in Number Sense

1. In a class of 62 children, 17 are boys. How many girls are in the class?
Show your work. How can you check your answer using addition?

2. This table shows the lengths of the Great Lakes.

Lake	Length
Lake Ontario	120 miles
Lake Superior	217 miles
Lake Michigan	191 miles
Lake Huron	128 miles
Lake Erie	150 miles

   a) Write the lengths in order from shortest to longest.

   b) How much longer than Lake Huron is Lake Michigan?

   c) How much longer than the shortest lake is the longest lake?

3. Use the numbers 1, 2, 3, 4, 5, 6 to make the greatest sum possible and the greatest difference possible.

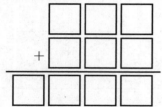 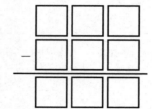

4. Find the error in Ezra's sum.

```
  2
  4 5
+ 2 7
─────
  8 1
```

5. Leonardo da Vinci, the great Italian inventor and artist, lived from 1452 to 1519.

   a) How old was he when he died?

   b) Leonardo painted his masterpiece the *Mona Lisa* in 1503. How old was he then?

6. Write the number that is ...

   a) ten less than 1,000

   b) ten more than 1,000

   c) 100 less than 1,000

   d) 100 more than 1,000

7. Pens cost 49¢. Erasers cost 45¢. Ben has 95¢. Does he have enough money to buy a pen and an eraser? Justify your answer.

8. Josh wants to add the numbers below. He starts by adding the ones digits. Explain why Josh wrote the number 1 above the 3 in 35.

Explain why Josh wrote ⟶
the number 1 here

```
    1
    3 5
  + 4 7
  ─────
      2
```

9. The table gives the area of some of the largest islands in North America.

a) How much greater than the area of the smallest island is the area of the largest island?

b) How much greater is the area of Ellesmere Island than Newfoundland?

Island	Area in square miles
Baffin Island	195,928
Ellesmere Island	75,769
Newfoundland	42,031
Cuba	40,543

10. Use each of the digits 4, 5, 6, 7, 8 once to create …

a) the greatest odd number possible.

b) a number between 56,700 and 57,000.

c) an even number whose tens digit and hundreds digit add to 12.

d) a number as close to 70,000 as possible (explain how you know your answer is correct).

11. There are 321,212 species of plants and 1,234,400 species of animals.

How many more species of animals are there than plants?

12. Use the numbers 1, 2, 3, 4 once in each problem.

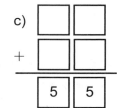

a)

$$
\begin{array}{ccc}
 & \square & \square \\
+ & 2 & \square \\
\hline
 & \square & 6 \\
\end{array}
$$

b)

$$
\begin{array}{ccc}
 & \square & \square \\
- & \square & \square \\
\hline
 & 1 & 1 \\
\end{array}
$$

c)

$$
\begin{array}{ccc}
 & \square & \square \\
+ & \square & \square \\
\hline
 & 5 & 5 \\
\end{array}
$$

d)

$$
\begin{array}{ccc}
\square & \square & \square \\
 & & \square \\
\hline
1 & 2 & 8 \\
\end{array}
$$

e)

$$
\begin{array}{ccc}
 & 4 & \square \\
+ & \square & \square \\
\hline
 & 6 & \square \\
\end{array}
$$

f)

$$
\begin{array}{ccc}
 & \square & \square \\
- & \square & \square \\
\hline
 & & 7 \\
\end{array}
$$

13. Here are some important events in the history of science.

- In 1543, Copernicus published a book claiming the Sun is the center of our solar system.
- In 1610, Galileo Galilei used his newly invented telescope to discover the moons of Jupiter.
- In 1667, Isaac Newton announced his law of gravity.

a) How long ago did Copernicus publish his book?

b) How many years passed between each event?

18. Multiplying by Adding On

Marisol knows how to find 3×6 by adding three 6s ($6 + 6 + 6 = 18$). Her teacher asks her how she can find 4×6 *quickly* (without adding four 6s).

Marisol knows that 4×6 is one more 6 than 3×6. She shows this in two ways:

With a picture

four 6s ⎰ ⎱ three 6s
plus one more 6

three 6s   plus one more 6

By adding

$4 \times 6 = 6 + 6 + 6 + 6$

Marisol knows that $\mathbf{4 \times 6 = 3 \times 6 + 6}$.

She knows $3 \times 6 = 18$, so $4 \times 6 = 18 + 6 = 24$.

1. Write a product for each array.

a) 4×3
rows | dots in each row

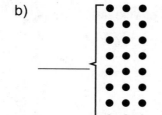
b)

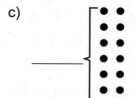
c)

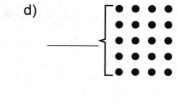
d)

2. Fill in the missing products and number.

a) 4×5
rows | dots in each row
3×5
$+ \underline{\ 5\ }$

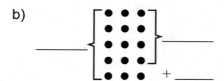
b)
$+ \underline{\hspace{1cm}}$

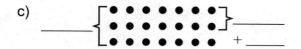
c)
$+ \underline{\hspace{1cm}}$

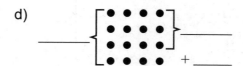
d)
$+ \underline{\hspace{1cm}}$

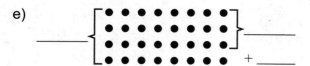
e)
$+ \underline{\hspace{1cm}}$

f)
$+ \underline{\hspace{1cm}}$

3. Fill in the missing products and number. Then write an equation.

a)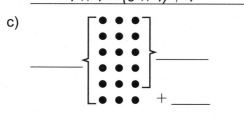

4×4 ⎨ 3×4
$+ \quad 4$

$\underline{\quad 4 \times 4 = (3 \times 4) + 4 \quad}$

b)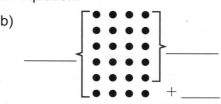

_____ ⎨ _____
$+$ _____

_____

c)

_____ ⎨ _____
$+$ _____

_____

d)

_____ ⎨ _____
$+$ _____

_____

You can always turn a product into a smaller product and a sum.

$$5 \times 3 = (\mathbf{4} \times 3) + \mathbf{3}$$

take 1 away from 5   add an extra 3

$$9 \times 4 = (\mathbf{8} \times 4) + \mathbf{4}$$

take 1 away from 9   add an extra 4

---

4. Turn each product into a smaller product and a sum.

a) $4 \times 2 = (3 \times \underline{\quad 2 \quad}) + \underline{\quad 2 \quad}$

b) $5 \times 7 = (4 \times \underline{\qquad}) + \underline{\qquad}$

c) $8 \times 3 = (7 \times \underline{\qquad}) + \underline{\qquad}$

d) $3 \times 6 = (2 \times \underline{\qquad}) + \underline{\qquad}$

e) $7 \times 4 = (\underline{\qquad} \times \underline{\qquad}) + \underline{\qquad}$

f) $9 \times 6 = (\underline{\qquad} \times \underline{\qquad}) + \underline{\qquad}$

g) $5 \times 5 = \underline{\qquad\qquad\qquad\qquad}$

h) $8 \times 7 = \underline{\qquad\qquad\qquad\qquad}$

i) $7 \times 6 = \underline{\qquad\qquad\qquad\qquad}$

j) $6 \times 4 = \underline{\qquad\qquad\qquad\qquad}$

5. Find each answer by turning the product into a smaller product and a sum.

a) $5 \times 3 = \underline{\quad (4 \times 3) + 3 \quad}$

     $= \underline{\quad 12 + 3 \quad}$

     $= \underline{\quad 15 \quad}$

b) $6 \times 3 = \underline{\qquad\qquad}$

     $= \underline{\qquad\qquad}$

     $= \underline{\qquad}$

c) $6 \times 4 = \underline{\qquad\qquad}$

     $= \underline{\qquad\qquad}$

     $= \underline{\qquad}$

d) $4 \times 4 = \underline{\qquad\qquad}$

     $= \underline{\qquad\qquad}$

     $= \underline{\qquad}$

e) 6×6 f) 3×7 g) 7×5 h) 6×8

---

19. Multiplying Tens, Hundreds, and Thousands

To multiply 3 × 20, Christie makes 3 groups of 2 tens blocks (20 = 2 tens).

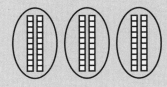

$3 \times 20 = 3 \times 2$ tens $= 6$ tens $= 60$

To multiply 3 × 200, Christie makes 3 groups of 2 hundreds blocks (200 = 2 hundreds).

$3 \times 200 = 3 \times 2$ hundreds $= 6$ hundreds $= 600$

Christie notices a pattern: $3 \times 2 = 6$ $3 \times 20 = 60$ $3 \times 200 = 600$

1. Draw a model for each multiplication statement, then calculate the answer.
   The first one is started for you.

   a) 4 × 20

   $4 \times 20 = 4 \times$ _____ tens $=$ _____ tens $=$ _____

   b) 2 × 30

   $2 \times 30 = 2 \times$ _____ tens $=$ _____ tens $=$ _____

2. Regroup to find the answer.

   a) $3 \times 70 = 3 \times$ __7__ tens $=$ __21__ tens $=$ __210__

   b) $3 \times 50 = 3 \times$ _____ tens $=$ _____ tens $=$ _____

   c) $5 \times 50 = 5 \times$ _____ tens $=$ _____ tens $=$ _____

   d) $4 \times 60 = 4 \times$ _____ tens $=$ _____ tens $=$ _____

3. Complete the pattern by multiplying.

   a) $2 \times 2 =$ _____   b) $5 \times 1 =$ _____   c) $2 \times 4 =$ _____   d) $3 \times 3 =$ _____

   $2 \times 20 =$ _____ $5 \times 10 =$ _____ $2 \times 40 =$ _____ $3 \times 30 =$ _____

   $2 \times 200 =$ _____ $5 \times 100 =$ _____ $2 \times 400 =$ _____ $3 \times 300 =$ _____

4. Multiply.

   a) $4 \times 30 =$ _____   b) $5 \times 30 =$ _____   c) $4 \times 40 =$ _____   d) $2 \times 50 =$ _____

   e) $3 \times 100 =$ _____   f) $4 \times 500 =$ _____   g) $3 \times 60 =$ _____   h) $6 \times 400 =$ _____

   i) $2 \times 700 =$ _____   j) $6 \times 70 =$ _____   k) $8 \times 40 =$ _____   l) $2 \times 900 =$ _____

5. Draw a base ten model to show 4 × 2,000.
   Use a cube to represent a thousand.

6. You know that 3 × 2 = 6. How can you use this fact to multiply 3 × 2,000?

$10 \times \square$ =

$10 \times$ | =

$10 \times \square$ =

10×1 one = 1 ten

10×1 ten = 1 hundred

10×1 hundred = 1 thousand

7. Draw a model for each multiplication statement, then calculate the answer.

a) $10 \times 30 = 10 \times$ ||| = $\square\square\square$ = _300_

b) $10 \times 200 = 10 \times$ $\square\square$ = = _____

c) $10 \times 40 = 10 \times$ |||| = = _____

d) $10 \times 5 = 10 \times$ ◻◻◻◻◻ = = _____

e) $10 \times 20 = 10 \times$ = = _____

f) $10 \times 4 = 10 \times$ = = _____

8. Multiply.

a) $10 \times 6 =$ _____

b) $10 \times 70 =$ _____

c) $10 \times 800 =$ _____

d) $10 \times 90 =$ _____

e) $10 \times 5 =$ _____

f) $10 \times 400 =$ _____

g) $10 \times 500 =$ _____

BONUS ▶ $10 \times 200{,}000{,}000 =$ _____

To multiply 20 × 60, Solmaz multiplies 2 × (10 × 60).
The picture shows why this works.

Two 10 × 60 rectangles make one 20 × 60 rectangle.

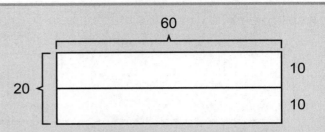

9. Multiply.

a) $20 \times 60 = 2 \times (10 \times 60)$
$= 2 \times \underline{\quad 600 \quad}$
$= \underline{\quad 1{,}200 \quad}$

b) $30 \times 500 = 3 \times (10 \times 500)$
$= 3 \times \underline{\qquad}$
$= \underline{\qquad}$

c) $40 \times 800 = 4 \times (10 \times 800)$
$= 4 \times \underline{\qquad}$
$= \underline{\qquad}$

d) $30 \times 80 = 3 \times (10 \times 80)$
$= 3 \times \underline{\qquad}$
$= \underline{\qquad}$

e) $70 \times 600 = 7 \times (10 \times 600)$
$= 7 \times \underline{\qquad}$
$= \underline{\qquad}$

f) $60 \times 700 = 6 \times (10 \times 700)$
$= 6 \times \underline{\qquad}$
$= \underline{\qquad}$

To multiply 40 × 700:
Step 1: Multiply 4 × 7 = 28.
Step 2: Write all the zeros from 40 and 700 in the answer: **40 × 700 = 28,000**.

10. Multiply the 1-digit numbers to multiply the tens and hundreds.

a) $8 \times 5 = \underline{\quad 40 \quad}$
$800 \times 50 = \underline{\quad 40{,}000 \quad}$

b) $2 \times 3 = \underline{\qquad}$
$20 \times 300 = \underline{\qquad}$

c) $5 \times 2 = \underline{\qquad}$
$50 \times 200 = \underline{\qquad}$

d) $8 \times 7 = \underline{\qquad}$
$800 \times 70 = \underline{\qquad}$

e) $4 \times 9 = \underline{\qquad}$
$40 \times 9{,}000 = \underline{\qquad}$

f) $5 \times 6 = \underline{\qquad}$
$500 \times 600 = \underline{\qquad}$

g) $40 \times 30 = \underline{\qquad}$

h) $300 \times 50 = \underline{\qquad}$

i) $80 \times 500 = \underline{\qquad}$

j) $800 \times 900 = \underline{\qquad}$

k) $50 \times 5{,}000 = \underline{\qquad}$

l) $40 \times 50{,}000 = \underline{\qquad}$

BONUS ▶ $3{,}000 \times 80{,}000 = \underline{\hspace{5cm}}$

11. a) Calculate each product on a calculator.

i) $3{,}142 \times 608$
$= \underline{\hspace{3cm}}$

ii) $2{,}984 \times 497$
$= \underline{\hspace{3cm}}$

iii) $70{,}162 \times 811$
$= \underline{\hspace{3cm}}$

b) Use estimation by rounding to check if your answers in part a) make sense.
Explain how you know. Use words such as "close to," "higher than," and
"lower than."

20. Mental Math

1. Write a product for each array.

a)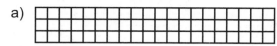

$\underline{\quad 3 \times 20 \quad}$

b)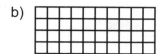

$\underline{\qquad\qquad}$

c)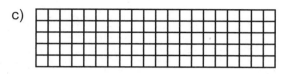

$\underline{\qquad\qquad}$

d)

$\underline{\qquad\qquad}$

2. Write a product for the whole array and for each part of the array (as shown in part a).

a)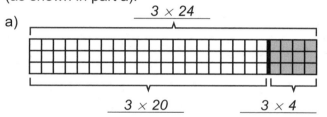

$\underline{\quad 3 \times 20 \quad}$ $\underline{\quad 3 \times 4 \quad}$

b)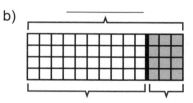

$\underline{\qquad}$ $\underline{\qquad}$

c)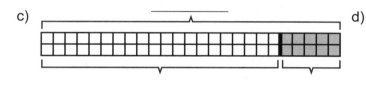

$\underline{\qquad}$ $\underline{\qquad}$

d)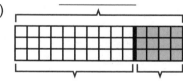

$\underline{\qquad}$ $\underline{\qquad}$

3. Fill in the blanks (as shown in part a).

a)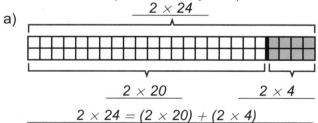

$\underline{\quad 2 \times 20 \quad}$ $\underline{\quad 2 \times 4 \quad}$

$\underline{2 \times 24 = (2 \times 20) + (2 \times 4)}$

b)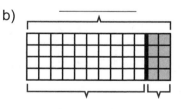

$\underline{\qquad}$

$\underline{\qquad\qquad\qquad\qquad}$

c)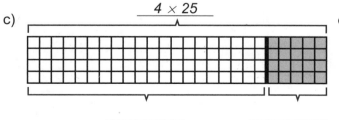

$\underline{\qquad}$ $\underline{\qquad}$

$\underline{\qquad\qquad\qquad\qquad}$

d)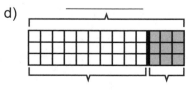

$\underline{\qquad}$ $\underline{\qquad}$

$\underline{\qquad\qquad\qquad\qquad}$

To multiply 3 × 23, Rosa rewrites 23 as a sum:

23 = 20 + 3

She multiplies 20 by 3 and then she multiplies 3 by 3:

3 × 20 = 60 and 3 × 3 = 9

Finally she adds the results: 60 + 9 = 69

The picture shows why Rosa's method works:

3 × 23 = (3 × 20) + (3 × 3) = 60 + 9 = 69

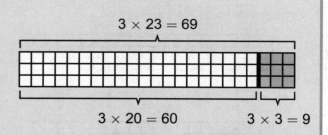

3 × 23 = 69

3 × 20 = 60   3 × 3 = 9

4. Rewrite each multiplication statement as a sum.

   a) 2 × 24 = ___ *2 × 20* ___ + ___ *2 × 4* ___   b) 2 × 23 = _____ + _____

   c) 3 × 32 = _____ + _____   d) 4 × 12 = _____ + _____

5. Multiply using Rosa's method.

   a) 3 × 13 = ___ *3 × 10* ___ + ___ *3 × 3* ___ = ___ *30 + 9* ___ = ___ *39* ___

   b) 3 × 21 = _____ + _____ = _____ = _____

   c) 2 × 14 = _____ + _____ = _____ = _____

   d) 3 × 213 = ___ *3 × 200* ___ + ___ *3 × 10* ___ + ___ *3 × 3* ___ = ___ *600 + 30 + 9* ___ = ___ *639* ___

   e) 2 × 231 = _____ + _____ + _____ = _____ = _____

   f) 2 × 342 = _____ + _____ + _____ = _____ = _____

6. Multiply in your head by multiplying the digits separately.

   a) 3 × 12 = _____   b) 2 × 31 = _____   c) 4 × 12 = _____   d) 5 × 11 = _____

   e) 4 × 21 = _____   f) 2 × 43 = _____   g) 2 × 32 = _____   h) 3 × 33 = _____

   i) 4 × 112 = _____   j) 2 × 234 = _____   k) 3 × 233 = _____   l) 5 × 111 = _____

   m) 3 × 132 = _____   n) 2 × 422 = _____   o) 4 × 212 = _____   p) 3 × 333 = _____

7. Yen planted 223 trees in each of 3 rows. How many trees did she plant altogether?

8. Paul put 240 marbles in each of 2 bags. How many marbles did he put in the bags?

21. Standard Method for Multiplication (No Regrouping)

Clara uses a chart to multiply 3 × 42:

Step 1: She multiplies the ones digit of 42 by 3. (3 × 2 = 6)

Step 2: She multiplies the tens digit of 42 by 3. (3 × 4 tens = 12 tens)

She regroups 10 tens → 1 2 6
as 1 hundred.
hundreds   tens

1. Use Clara's method to find the products.

a)
```
    3 1
×     4
```

b)
```
    5 3
×     2
```

c)
```
    4 1
×     4
```

d)
```
    2 1
×     6
```

e)
```
    3 1
×     3
```

f)
```
    7 1
×     2
```

g)
```
    6 2
×     3
```

h)
```
    8 4
×     2
```

i)
```
    5 2
×     4
```

j)
```
    2 2
×     2
```

k)
```
    2 1
×     5
```

l)
```
    5 3
×     3
```

m)
```
    4 2
×     4
```

n)
```
    4 3
×     3
```

o)
```
    6 4
×     2
```

p)
```
    7 3
×     3
```

q)
```
    5 4
×     2
```

r)
```
    6 2
×     4
```

s)
```
    7 2
×     3
```

t)
```
    9 1
×     2
```

u)
```
    6 3
×     3
```

v)
```
    8 1
×     2
```

w)
```
    5 1
×     5
```

x)
```
    7 2
×     4
```

y)
```
    6 1
×     5
```

z)
```
    7 2
×     2
```

aa)
```
    8 3
×     3
```

bb)
```
    9 1
×     9
```

cc)
```
    4 1
×     6
```

dd)
```
    6 1
×     8
```

ee)
```
    9 2
×     4
```

ff)
```
    8 5
×     1
```

gg)
```
    4 3
×     2
```

hh)
```
    6 1
×     7
```

ii)
```
    7 1
×     8
```

2. Find the following products.

a) 2 × 62   b) 2 × 74   c) 4 × 21   d) 4 × 62   e) 5 × 41   f) 7 × 21

22. Multiplication with Regrouping

Leo uses a chart to multiply 3 × 24:

Step 1: He multiplies 4 ones by 3. (4 × 3 = 12)

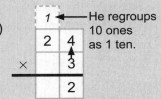

He regroups 10 ones as 1 ten.

Step 2: He multiplies 2 tens by 3. (3 × 2 tens = 6 tens)

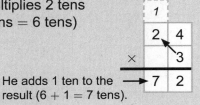

He adds 1 ten to the result (6 + 1 = 7 tens).

1. Using Leo's method, complete the first step of the multiplication.

a)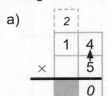
b)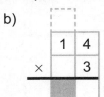
c)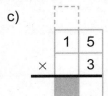
d)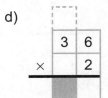
e)

2. Using Leo's method, complete the second step of the multiplication.

a)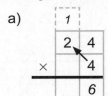
b)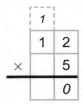
c)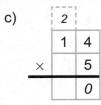
d)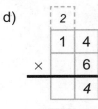
e)

f)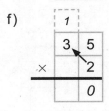
g)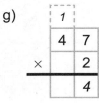
h)
i)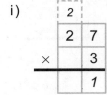
j)

3. Using Leo's method, complete the first and second steps of the multiplication.

a)
b)
c)
d)
e)

f)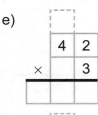
g)
h)
i)
j)

23. Multiplying with the 6, 7, 8, and 9 Times Tables

1. Finish the 3 times table. Double the 3 times table to write the 6 times table.

	1	2	3	4	5	6	7	8	9
the number × 3	3	6	9						
the number × 6	6	12	18						

2. Multiply by 6.

a) 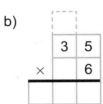   b) 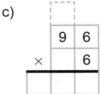   c) 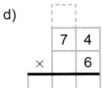   d)   e)

f) 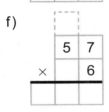   g) 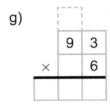   h) 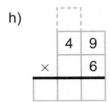   i) 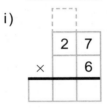   j)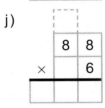

3. Cover the top of this page and multiply. Use grid paper to line up the place values.

a) 37 × 6   b) 98 × 6   c) 79 × 6   d) 85 × 6   e) 46 × 6

4. Finish the 2 times table. Double the 2 times table to write the 4 times table. Then double again to write the 8 times table.

	1	2	3	4	5	6	7	8	9
the number × 2	2	4	6						
the number × 4	4	8	12						
the number × 8	8	16	24						

5. Multiply by 8.

a) 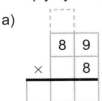   b) 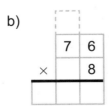   c) 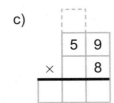   d) 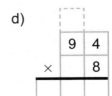   e)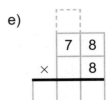

6. Multiply by 8. Only look at the times table when you need to. Use grid paper to line up the place values.

    a) 99 × 8   b) 69 × 8   c) 68 × 8   d) 87 × 8   e) 77 × 8

7. Continue the pattern in the tens digits and the ones digits to write the 9 times table.

    1 × 9 = _____ _9_   6 × 9 = _____ _____

    2 × 9 = _1_   _8_   7 × 9 = _____ _____

    3 × 9 = _2_   _7_   8 × 9 = _____ _____

    4 × 9 = _____ _____   9 × 9 = _____ _____

    5 × 9 = _____ _____   10 × 9 = _____ _____

8. Multiply by 9.

a) 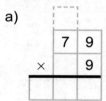 b) 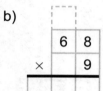 c) 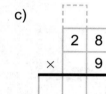 d) 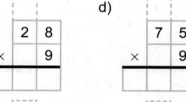 e)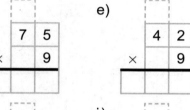

f) 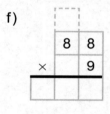 g) 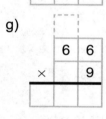 h) 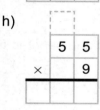 i) 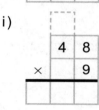 j)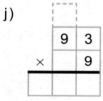

REMINDER ▶ If you know 7 × 9, then you know 9 × 7 too.

---

9. Use 7 × 7 = 49 and all the other times tables to write the 7 times table.

	1	2	3	4	5	6	7	8	9
the number × 7									

10. Use grid paper to multiply by 7. Only use the times table when you need to.

    a) 36 × 7   b) 48 × 7   c) 27 × 7   d) 81 × 7   e) 18 × 7

    f) 85 × 7   g) 76 × 7   h) 59 × 7   i) 94 × 7   j) 39 × 7

---

24. Multiplying a Multi-Digit Number by a 1-Digit Number

Kim multiplies 2×213 in three different ways.

1. With a chart:

hundreds	tens	ones
2	1	3
×		2
4	2	6

2. In expanded form:

$$200 + 10 + 3$$
$$\times\ 2$$
$$= 400 + 20 + 6$$
$$= 426$$

3. With base ten materials:

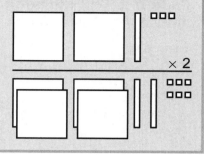

1. Rewrite the multiplication in expanded form. Then multiply.

a) 321   _____ + _____ + _____   b) 432   _____ + _____ + _____
    × 3   _____   × 3   × 2   _____   × 2

    = _____ + _____ + _____   = _____ + _____ + _____

    = _____   = _____

2. Draw a picture to show the result of the multiplication.

a) 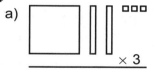   b) 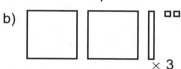   c)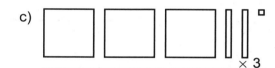

3. Multiply.

a)
1	2	4
×		2

b)
2	1	3
×		3

c)
1	2	2
×		4

d)
3	2	3
×		3

e)
4	1	3
×		2

4. Multiply by regrouping ones as tens.

a) *1*
1	2	3
×		4
4	9	2

b)
3	2	5
×		3

c)
1	1	4
×		5

d)
3	1	6
×		2

e)
1	1	5
×		6

5. Multiply by regrouping tens as hundreds.

a)
2	4	1
×		4

b)
1	5	1
×		5

c)
2	4	2
×		3

d)
1	5	2
×		3

e)
2	5	3
×		3

6. Copy these questions onto grid paper. Multiply by regrouping where you need to.

a) 347×2 b) 263×3 c) 117×5 d) 232×4 e) 172×4 f) 317×3

Sometimes, you need to regroup hundreds as thousands. When there are no other thousands, you don't need to show the regrouping on top—you can put the regrouping in the answer right away.

Example:  You don't need to write this 2 here, because there are no other thousands to add to it.

---

7. a) Circle the products you expect to be greater than 1,000.

i) 841×2 ii) 283×3 iii) 731×5 iv) 916×4 v) 237×4

b) Multiply by regrouping where you need to.

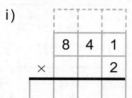 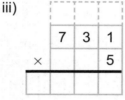 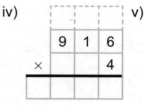 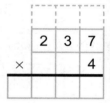

c) Were your predictions in part a) correct? If not, was the mistake in your calculation or your estimation strategy?

Sometimes you need to regroup two or three times.

Example 1:    Example 2:

---

8. Multiply. You will need to copy questions f) to j) onto grid paper.

a)    b) 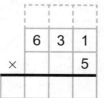   c)    d)    e)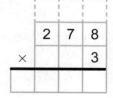

f) 4×247 g) 5×841 h) 7×213 i) 8×134 j) 3×738

---

9. Complete the 6, 7, 8, and 9 times tables.

	1	2	3	4	5	6	7	8	9
the number × 6									
the number × 7									
the number × 8									
the number × 9									

10. Multiply by regrouping where you need to.

a)
```
    5  8  1  3
×            6
─────────────
```

b)
```
    2  8  0  9
×            7
─────────────
```

c)
```
    9  6  8  7
×            8
─────────────
```

d)
```
    8  0  7  9
×            8
─────────────
```

e)
```
    8  6  1  5
×            6
─────────────
```

f)
```
    9  7  1  3
×            7
─────────────
```

g)
```
    9  6  8  7
×            9
─────────────
```

BONUS ▶
```
    8  5  4  3  9  0  2  6  1  7
×                              8
──────────────────────────────
```

11. An octopus has 8 arms and 240 suckers on each arm. How many suckers does an octopus have?

12. Kim can read 1,037 words in an hour. How many words can she read in 8 hours?

13. A factory produces 2,847 Popsicles in a day. How many Popsicles does the factory produce in 6 days?

14. Michael made 1,842 shirts. Each shirt has 7 buttons. How many buttons did he use?

25. Word Problems with Multiplying

1. Ron bikes 10,372 yards each day. How many yards does he bike in four days?

2. On average, every American uses 147 gallons of water each day.

    a) About how much water does each American use in a week?

    b) About how much water would a family of 4 use in a day?

3. a) The product of 3 and 2 is 6 because $3 \times 2 = 6$. The sum of 3 and 2 is 5 because $3 + 2 = 5$. Which is greater: the sum or the product?

    b) Try finding the sum and the product of different pairs of numbers. (For example, try 3 and 4, 2 and 5, 5 and 6, 1 and 7.) What do you notice? Is the product always greater than the sum?

4. Elisa multiplied two numbers, both not zero. The product was one of the numbers. What was the other number?

5. Write all the pairs of numbers you can think of that multiply to give 20.
BONUS ▶ Find all pairs of numbers that multiply to give 40.

cicada

6. A cicada can burrow into the ground and stay there for 10 years.

    a) How many months can a cicada stay in the ground?

    b) Sometimes, cicadas stay in the ground for up to 20 years. How can you use your answer in part a) to find out how many months this is?

7. There are 4 ways to put 6 dots into arrays so that each row contains the same number of dots.

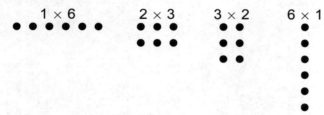

How many ways can you put each number of dots into one or more equal rows? Write a multiplication statement for each array.

    a) 4 dots   b) 8 dots   c) 12 dots   d) 16 dots

8. Roger rode a horse around a six-sided field with each side 355 yards long. How far did he ride?

26. Multiplying 2-Digit Numbers by Multiples of 10

Erin wants to multiply 20×32. She knows how to find 2×32.
She rewrites 20×32 as $(10 \times 2) \times 32$:

$$20 \times 32 = (10 \times 2) \times 32$$
$$= 10 \times (2 \times 32)$$
$$= 10 \times 64$$
$$= 640$$

The picture shows why this works:
    a 20×32 array contains the same number
    of squares as ten 2×32 arrays.

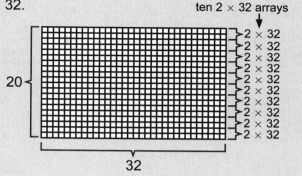

ten 2×32 arrays

20⟨ ... ⟩ 2×32 (×10)

32

---

1. Rewrite the product using Erin's method.

   a) $20 \times 33 = \underline{\ 10 \times (2 \times 33)\ }$ b) $20 \times 22 = \underline{\hspace{3cm}}$

   c) $30 \times 13 = \underline{\hspace{3cm}}$ d) $50 \times 41 = \underline{\hspace{3cm}}$

2. Find the product.

   a) $40 \times 12 = \underline{\ 10\ } \times (\ \underline{\ 4\ } \times \underline{\ 12\ }\ )$ b) $60 \times 21 = \underline{\hspace{1cm}} \times (\ \underline{\hspace{1cm}} \times \underline{\hspace{1cm}}\ )$

                   $= \underline{\ 10 \times 48\ }$ $= \underline{\hspace{2cm}}$

                   $= \underline{\ 480\ }$ $= \underline{\hspace{1.5cm}}$

   c) $40 \times 22 = \underline{\hspace{1cm}} \times (\ \underline{\hspace{1cm}} \times \underline{\hspace{1cm}}\ )$ d) $50 \times 31 = \underline{\hspace{1cm}} \times (\ \underline{\hspace{1cm}} \times \underline{\hspace{1cm}}\ )$

                   $= \underline{\hspace{2cm}}$ $= \underline{\hspace{2cm}}$

                   $= \underline{\hspace{1.5cm}}$ $= \underline{\hspace{1.5cm}}$

3. Find the product mentally.

   a) $30 \times 22 = \underline{\hspace{1.5cm}}$ b) $20 \times 40 = \underline{\hspace{1.5cm}}$ c) $20 \times 60 = \underline{\hspace{1.5cm}}$ d) $40 \times 32 = \underline{\hspace{1.5cm}}$

   e) $20 \times 41 = \underline{\hspace{1.5cm}}$ f) $30 \times 92 = \underline{\hspace{1.5cm}}$ g) $51 \times 20 = \underline{\hspace{1.5cm}}$ h) $30 \times 63 = \underline{\hspace{1.5cm}}$

   i) $60 \times 41 = \underline{\hspace{1.5cm}}$ j) $61 \times 50 = \underline{\hspace{1.5cm}}$ k) $70 \times 30 = \underline{\hspace{1.5cm}}$ l) $80 \times 20 = \underline{\hspace{1.5cm}}$

4. Estimate the product. Hint: Round each number to the nearest ten.

   a) $27 \times 39 \approx \underline{\ 30 \times 40 = \ \ 1{,}200\ }$ b) $43 \times 51 \approx \underline{\hspace{3cm}}$

   c) $22 \times 47 \approx \underline{\hspace{3cm}}$ d) $62 \times 41 \approx \underline{\hspace{3cm}}$

   e) $72 \times 49 \approx \underline{\hspace{3cm}}$ f) $38 \times 17 \approx \underline{\hspace{3cm}}$

5. Find the product.

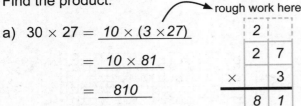

a) $30 \times 27 = \underline{10 \times (3 \times 27)}$
$ = \underline{10 \times 81}$
$ = \underline{810}$

rough work here

b) $50 \times 15 = \underline{} \times (\underline{} \times \underline{})$
$ = \underline{}$
$ = \underline{}$

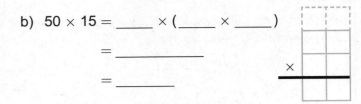

c) $30 \times 24 = \underline{} \times (\underline{} \times \underline{})$
$ = \underline{}$
$ = \underline{}$

d) $40 \times 15 = \underline{} \times (\underline{} \times \underline{})$
$ = \underline{}$
$ = \underline{}$

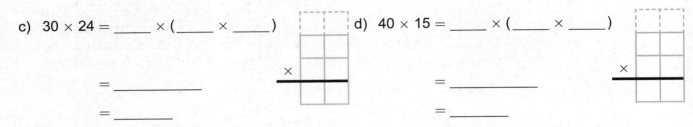

You can use a chart to find $40 \times 57 = 10 \times (4 \times 57)$.

Step 1: $10 \times (4 \times 57)$
When you multiply a number by 10, you add a zero. So write a zero in the ones place because you will multiply (4×57) by 10.

Steps 2 and 3: $10 \times (\mathbf{4 \times 57})$
Now multiply 57 by 4.

Regroup the 2 in the hundreds place because you are really multiplying 7 by 40, not 4.

6. Practice the first two steps of the multiplication. Note: In one of the problems, you will not need to regroup the hundreds.

a)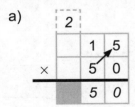

b)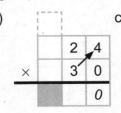

c)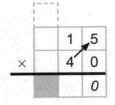

d)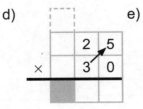

e)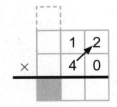

7. Multiply.

a)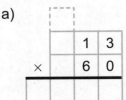

b)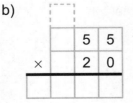

c)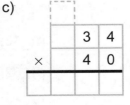

d)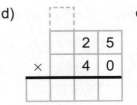

e)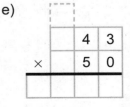

f) 28×30 g) 36×20 h) 27×40 i) 23×60 j) 43×70

JUMP Math Accumula

27. Multiplying 2-Digit Numbers by 2-Digit Numbers

To multiply 37×25, split 25 into two numbers that are easier to multiply by. The picture shows why this works.

a multiple of 10   a 1-digit number

$$37 \times 25 = 37 \times \mathbf{20} + 37 \times \mathbf{5}$$
$$= 740 + 185$$
$$= 925$$

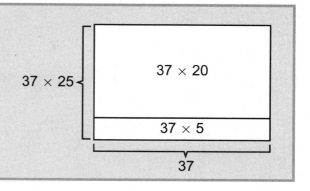

1. Find each product by rewriting the second number as the sum of a 1-digit number and a multiple of 10.

add here

a) 65×27

$$= \underline{\quad 65 \times (\ 20 \ + \ 7 \ ) \quad}$$
$$= \underline{\quad 65 \times 20 + 65 \times 7 \quad}$$
$$= \underline{\quad 1{,}300 + 455 \quad}$$
$$= \underline{\quad 1{,}755 \quad}$$

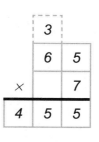 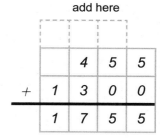

b) 54×23

$$= \underline{\quad} \times (\underline{\quad} + \underline{\quad})$$
$$= \underline{\qquad\qquad}$$
$$= \underline{\qquad\qquad}$$
$$= \underline{\qquad\qquad}$$

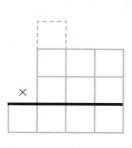 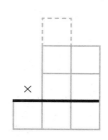 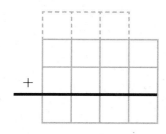

c) 81×27

$$= \underline{\quad} \times (\underline{\quad} + \underline{\quad})$$
$$= \underline{\qquad\qquad}$$
$$= \underline{\qquad\qquad}$$
$$= \underline{\qquad\qquad}$$

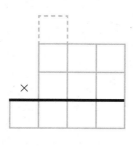 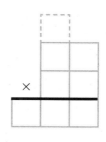 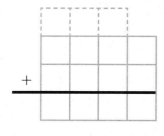

d) 72×45

$$= \underline{\qquad\qquad}$$
$$= \underline{\qquad\qquad}$$
$$= \underline{\qquad\qquad}$$
$$= \underline{\qquad\qquad}$$

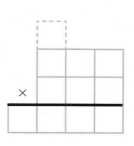 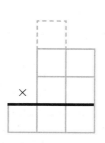 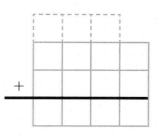

You can record the steps in multiplying 2-digit numbers on a grid.

Example: Find 37×25.

Step 1: Calculate 37×5.

Step 2: Calculate 37×20.

Step 3: Add the results.

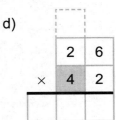

$\leftarrow 37 \times 5$

$\leftarrow 37 \times 20$

2. Practice Step 1.

a)

	1	
	1	4
×	3	4
	5	6

$= 14 \times 4$

b)

	2	3
×	1	5

$= 5 \times 23$

c)

	2	4
×	1	3

d)

	2	6
×	4	2

e)

	3	4
×	1	3

f)

	2	5
×	4	2

g)

	3	6
×	4	2

h)

	2	4
×	4	5

3. Practice Step 2.

a)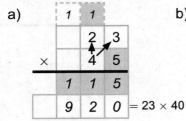

$= 23 \times 40$

b)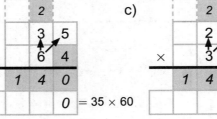

$= 35 \times 60$

c)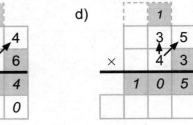

d)

e)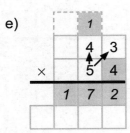

f)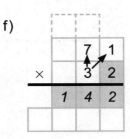

g)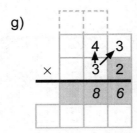

h)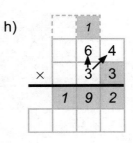

JUMP Math Accumula

4. Practice Steps 1 and 2.

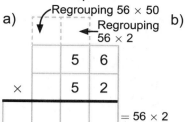

a) Regrouping 56 × 50 | Regrouping 56 × 2

	5	6
×	5	2
			= 56 × 2
	0		= 56 × 50

b)

	3	5
×	2	6

c)

	2	5
×	3	7

d)

	2	3
×	3	4

e)

	6	5
×	4	3

f)

	4	5
×	3	2

g)

	3	3
×	4	4

h)

	1	5
×	4	6

5. Complete the multiplication by adding the numbers in the last two rows of the chart.

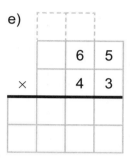 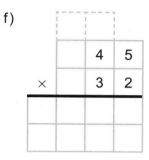 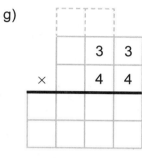

a)

		1	
		1	2
×		3	8
		9	6
+	3	6	0
	4	5	6

b)

	1	4	
		2	8
×		2	6
	1	6	8
+	5	6	0

c)

	4	2	
		5	7
×		6	3
	1	7	1
+	3	4	2	0

d)

		8	1
×		3	5
	4	0	5
+	2	4	3	0

6. Multiply.

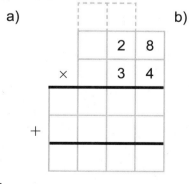 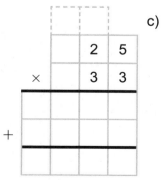

a)

	2	8
×	3	4
+		

b)

	2	5
×	3	3
+		

c)

	4	3
×	5	2
+		

d)

	6	3
×	2	7
+		

7. Find the products.

a) 27 × 32   b) 56 × 73   c) 85 × 64   d) 19 × 93   e) 74 × 86   f) 64 × 98

28. Topics in Multiplication

1. Kyle has 2 stickers. Ravi has 8 stickers.

   Ravi has _____ times as many stickers as Kyle.

2. A bee has 6 legs. How many legs do 325 bees have?

3. A harp has 47 strings. How many strings do 12 harps have?

4. Explain why the product of two 2-digit numbers must be at least 100.

   _____

   _____

5. A hummingbird flaps its wings 15 times a second. How many times does it flap its wings in a minute?

6. How many hours are there in the month of January?

7. Use the digits 3, 4, and 5 to make …

   a) the greatest product

   □ × □□

   b) the least product

   □ × □□

8. Use the digits 1, 2, 3, and 4 to make …

   a) the greatest product

   □ × □□□

   b) the least product

   □ × □□□

9. Find the first four products. Use the pattern in the products to find the products in parts e) and f) without multiplying.

a)		3	7
×			9

b)		3	7
×		1	2
+			

c)		3	7
×		1	5
+			

d)		3	7
×		1	8
+			

e)		3	7
×		2	1

f)		3	7
×		2	4

10. Find the products.

    a) $0 \times 5 =$ _____

    b) $0 \times 7 =$ _____

    c) $0 \times 9 =$ _____

    d) $17 \times 0 =$ _____

11. Erin multiplied a number by 5 and got 0. What was the original number? _____

29. Sets and Sharing

Elisa has 12 glasses of water. A tray holds 3 glasses. There are 4 trays.

Question:

What has been shared or divided into **sets** or **groups**?
How many sets are there?
How many of the things being divided are in each set?

Answer:

Glasses
There are 4 sets of glasses.
There are 3 glasses in each set.

1. a)

   What has been shared or divided into sets?

   _____

   How many sets? _____

   How many in each set? _____

   b)

   What has been shared or divided into sets?

   _____

   How many sets? _____

   How many in each set? _____

2. Using *circles* for sets and *dots* for things, draw a picture to show …

   a) 4 sets
      6 things in each set

   b) 6 groups
      3 things in each group

   c) 6 sets
      2 things in each set

   d) 4 groups
      5 things in each group

3. Complete the table.

		What has been shared or divided into sets?	How many sets?	How many in each set?
a)	20 toys 4 toys for each child 5 children	20 toys	5	4
b)	7 friends 21 pencils 3 pencils for each friend			
c)	16 students 4 desks 4 students at each desk			
d)	8 plants 24 flowers 3 flowers on each plant			
e)	6 grapefruits in each box 42 grapefruits 7 boxes			
f)	3 school buses 30 children 10 children in each school bus			
g)	6 puppies in each litter 6 litters 36 puppies			
h)	28 markers 4 kids 7 markers for each kid			
i)	4 boxes 24 markers 6 markers in each box			

BONUS ▶ Draw pictures for Questions 3 a), b), and c) using *circles* for sets and *dots* for the things being divided.

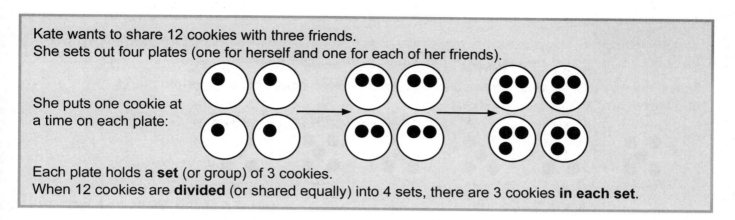

Kate wants to share 12 cookies with three friends.
She sets out four plates (one for herself and one for each of her friends).

She puts one cookie at a time on each plate:

Each plate holds a **set** (or group) of 3 cookies.
When 12 cookies are **divided** (or shared equally) into 4 sets, there are 3 cookies **in each set**.

4. Put an equal number of cookies on each plate the way Kate did.
   Draw the plates, then place one cookie at a time.

   a) 12 cookies; 3 plates

   b) 16 cookies; 4 plates

5. Draw dots for the things being shared or divided equally. Draw circles for the sets.

   a) 2 vans; 8 people
       How many people in each van?

   b) 3 kids; 9 stickers
       How many stickers for each kid?

   c) 20 flowers; 5 plants
       How many flowers on each plant?

   d) 12 grapefruits; 6 boxes
       How many grapefruits in each box?

6. Five friends shared 20 cherries equally. How many cherries did each friend get?

7. Eileen shared 20 stickers among 3 friends and herself. How many stickers did each person get?

8. There are 16 apples in 8 trees. How many apples are in each tree?

30. Sharing When You Know the Number in Each Set

Samuel has 30 apples. He wants to give 5 apples to each of his friends.

To find out how many friends he can give apples to, he counts out **sets** (or **groups**) of 5 apples until he has used all 30 apples.

He can give apples to 6 friends. When 30 apples are divided into sets of 5 apples, there are 6 sets.

1. Put the correct number of dots in each set. The first one has been done for you.

   a)

   4 dots in each set

   b) ● ● ● ● ● ● ● ● ● ●

   5 dots in each set

   c) ● ● ● ● ● ● ● ● ● ● ● ●

   3 dots in each set

2. Draw circles to divide these arrays into …

   a) groups of 3

   ● ● ●
   ● ● ●
   ● ● ●

   b) groups of 4

   ● ● ● ●
   ● ● ● ●
   ● ● ● ●

   c) groups of 3

   ● ● ● ● ●
   ● ● ● ● ●
   ● ● ● ● ●

   d) groups of 4

   ● ● ● ●
   ● ● ● ●
   ● ● ● ●
   ● ● ● ●

3. Draw dots for the things being shared or divided equally. Draw circles for the sets.

   a) 15 apples; 5 apples in each box
      How many boxes?

   b) 10 stickers; 2 stickers for each kid
      How many kids?

   _____ boxes

   _____ kids

4. Shelly has 18 cookies. She gives 3 cookies to each of her siblings.
   How many siblings does she have?

5. Mumtaz has 14 stamps. He puts 2 stamps on each envelope.
   How many envelopes does he have?

31. Two Ways of Sharing

Samuel has 15 cookies. There are two ways he can share or **divide** the cookies equally:

Method 1: Decide how many sets (or groups) **to make.**

Example: Samuel wants to make 3 sets of cookies. He draws 3 circles: He puts one cookie at a time into the circles until he has placed all 15 cookies.

Method 2: Decide how many will be in each set.

Example: Samuel wants to put 5 cookies in each set. He counts out 5 cookies: He counts out sets of 5 until he has placed all 15 cookies.

Use Method 1 to do Questions 1, 2, and 3.

1. Share **20** dots equally. How many dots are in each set? Hint: Place one dot at a time.

   a) 4 sets:

   There are _____ dots in each set.

   b) 5 sets:

   There are _____ dots in each set.

2. Share the triangles equally among the sets. Hint: Count the triangles first.

   a)

   b)

3. Share the squares equally among the sets.

Use Method 2 to do Questions 4 and 5.

4. Group the lines so that there are 3 lines in each set.

   a) | | | | | | | | |

   There are _____ sets.

   b) | | | | | | | | | | | |

   There are _____ sets.

   c) | | | | | |

   There are _____ sets.

5. Group **12** dots so that …

   a) there are 6 dots in each set.

   b) there are 4 dots in each set.

6. For each part, fill in what you know. Write a question mark for what you don't know.

		What has been shared or divided into sets?	How many sets?	How many in each set?
a)	Vanessa has 25 pencils. She puts 5 pencils in each box.	25 pencils	?	5
b)	30 children are in 10 boats.	30 children	10	?
c)	Ben has 36 stickers. He gives 9 stickers to each of his friends.			
d)	Donald has 12 books. He puts 3 on each shelf.			
e)	15 girls sit at 3 tables.			
f)	30 students are in 2 school buses.			
g)	9 fruit bars are shared among 3 children.			
h)	15 chairs are in 3 rows.			
i)	Each basket holds 4 eggs. There are 12 eggs altogether.			

7. Draw a picture using dots and circles to solve each part of Question 6.

8. Draw a picture using dots and circles to show the answer.

a) 15 dots; 5 sets

_____ dots in each set

b) 16 dots; 8 dots in each set

_____ sets

c) 15 dots; 5 dots in each set

_____ sets

d) 8 dots; 4 sets

_____ dots in each set

e) 10 children are in 2 boats.

How many children are in each boat? _____

f) Paul has 12 pencils.
He puts 3 pencils in each box.

How many boxes does he have? _____

g) 4 boys share 12 marbles.

How many marbles does each boy get? _____

h) Pamela has 10 apples.
She gives 2 apples to each friend.

How many friends receive apples? _____

i) 6 children go sailing in 2 boats.

How many children are in each boat? _____

j) Alan has 10 stickers.
He puts 2 on each page.

How many pages does he use? _____

32. Division, Addition, and Multiplication

Every division equation can be rewritten as an *addition equation* and a *multiplication equation*.

Example: "15 divided into sets of size 3 equals 5 sets" gives

"adding 3 five times equals 15"   and   "5 groups of 3 equals 15"

$3 + 3 + 3 + 3 + 3 = 15$ $5 \times 3 = 15$

1. Draw a picture and write addition and multiplication equations for each division equation.

   a) $8 \div 2 = 4$ b) $12 \div 6 = 2$ c) $12 \div 3 = 4$

   $2 + 2 + 2 + 2 = 8$ _____ _____
   $4 \times 2 = 8$ _____ _____

2. Draw a picture and write a division equation for each multiplication or addition equation.

   a) $3 \times 4 = 12$ b) $3 \times 6 = 18$

   $12 \div 4 = 3$ _____

   c) $5 + 5 + 5 + 5 = 20$ d) $2 \times 5 = 10$

   _____   _____

   e) $5 \times 3 = 15$ f) $9 + 9 = 18$

   _____   _____

JUMP Math Accumula

33. Remainders

Ori wants to share 7 strawberries with 2 friends.
He sets out 3 plates, one for himself and one for each of his friends.
He puts one strawberry at a time on each plate:

There is one strawberry left over.

7 strawberries cannot be divided equally into 3 sets. Each friend gets 2 strawberries, but one is left over.

7 ÷ 3 = 2 Remainder 1

1. Can 2 people share 5 strawberries equally? Show your work using dots and circles.

2. Share the dots as equally as possible among the circles.
   Note: In one question, the dots can be shared equally (so there's no remainder).

   a) 7 dots in 2 circles

   b) 10 dots in 3 circles

   _____ dots in each circle; _____ dot remaining   _____ dots in each circle; _____ dot remaining

   c) 10 dots in 5 circles

   d) 9 dots in 4 circles

   _____ dots in each circle; _____ dots remaining   _____ dots in each circle; _____ dot remaining

   e) 12 dots in 5 circles

   f) 13 dots in 4 circles

   _____ dots in each circle; _____ dots remaining   _____ dots in each circle; _____ dot remaining

3. Share the dots as equally as possible. Draw a picture and write a division equation.

a) 7 dots in 3 circles

$7 \div 3 = 2$ *Remainder 1*

b) 11 dots in 3 circles

c) 14 dots in 3 circles

d) 10 dots in 6 circles

e) 10 dots in 4 circles

f) 13 dots in 5 circles

4. Three friends want to share 7 cherries. How many cherries will each friend receive? How many will be left over? Show your work and write a division equation.

5. Find two different ways to share 13 granola bars into equal groups so that one is left over.

6. Fred, George, and Paul have fewer than 10 oranges and more than 3 oranges. They share the oranges equally. How many oranges do they have? Is there more than one answer?

34. Finding Remainders on Number Lines

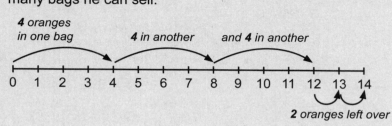

Paul has 14 oranges. He wants to sell them in bags of 4. He skip counts to find out how many bags he can sell.

4 oranges in one bag   *4 in another*   and *4 in another*

2 oranges left over

14 oranges divided into sets of size 4 gives 3 sets (with 2 oranges **remaining**)

14 ÷ 4 = 3 Remainder 2

Size of skip   Number of skips

1. Fill in the missing numbers.

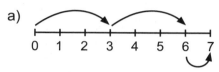

a)

0 1 2 3 4 5 6 7

Size of skip = _____

Number of skips = _____

Remainder = _____

b)

0 1 2 3 4 5 6 7

Size of skip = _____

Number of skips = _____

Remainder = _____

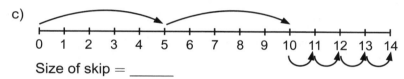

c)

0 1 2 3 4 5 6 7 8 9 10 11 12 13 14

Size of skip = _____

Number of skips = _____

Remainder = _____

2. Write the division equation.

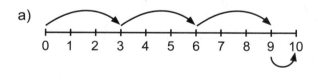

a)

0 1 2 3 4 5 6 7 8 9 10

_____

b)

0 1 2 3 4 5 6 7

_____

3. Jane has 11 oranges. She wants to make bags of 4.

How many bags can she make? _____

How many oranges will be left over? _____

0 1 2 3 4 5 6 7 8 9 10 11

4. On grid paper, draw a number line picture to show the division.

a) 5 ÷ 2 = 2 Remainder 1   b) 9 ÷ 4 = 2 Remainder 1   c) 11 ÷ 3 = 3 Remainder 2

Nina wants to find $13 \div 5$ mentally.

Step 1: Nina counts by 5s. She stops when counting more would pass 13.

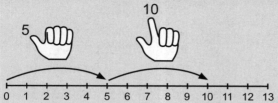

She has two fingers up.

$13 \div 5 = \underline{\ 2\ }$ Remainder $\underline{\hspace{2em}}$

Step 2: Nina stops counting at 10. She subtracts 10 from 13 to find the remainder.

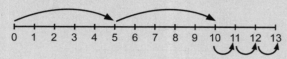

$13 \div 5 = \underline{\ 2\ }$ Remainder $\underline{\ 3\ }$

5. Divide by skip counting.

   a) $18 \div 5 = \underline{\hspace{3em}}$ R $\underline{\hspace{3em}}$
   b) $23 \div 5 = \underline{\hspace{3em}}$ R $\underline{\hspace{3em}}$
   c) $26 \div 5 = \underline{\hspace{3em}}$ R $\underline{\hspace{3em}}$

   d) $28 \div 5 = \underline{\hspace{3em}}$ R $\underline{\hspace{3em}}$
   e) $16 \div 5 = \underline{\hspace{3em}}$ R $\underline{\hspace{3em}}$
   f) $6 \div 5 = \underline{\hspace{3em}}$ R $\underline{\hspace{3em}}$

   g) $10 \div 3 = \underline{\hspace{3em}}$ R $\underline{\hspace{3em}}$
   h) $7 \div 3 = \underline{\hspace{3em}}$ R $\underline{\hspace{3em}}$
   i) $16 \div 3 = \underline{\hspace{3em}}$ R $\underline{\hspace{3em}}$

   j) $8 \div 2 = \underline{\hspace{3em}}$ R $\underline{\hspace{3em}}$
   k) $5 \div 2 = \underline{\hspace{3em}}$ R $\underline{\hspace{3em}}$
   l) $17 \div 4 = \underline{\hspace{3em}}$ R $\underline{\hspace{3em}}$

   m) $16 \div 7 = \underline{\hspace{3em}}$ R $\underline{\hspace{3em}}$
   n) $28 \div 9 = \underline{\hspace{3em}}$ R $\underline{\hspace{3em}}$
   o) $25 \div 8 = \underline{\hspace{3em}}$ R $\underline{\hspace{3em}}$

   p) $13 \div 2 = \underline{\hspace{3em}}$ R $\underline{\hspace{3em}}$
   q) $45 \div 8 = \underline{\hspace{3em}}$ R $\underline{\hspace{3em}}$
   r) $63 \div 7 = \underline{\hspace{3em}}$ R $\underline{\hspace{3em}}$

6. Richard wants to divide 16 pencils among 5 friends.

   How many pencils will each friend get? $\underline{\hspace{5em}}$

   How many will be left over? $\underline{\hspace{5em}}$

7. You have 17 tickets for rides at an amusement park. Each ride takes 5 tickets.

   How many rides can you go on? $\underline{\hspace{5em}}$

   How many tickets will be left over? $\underline{\hspace{5em}}$

35. Long Division—2-Digit by 1-Digit

Inez is preparing snacks for 4 classes. She needs to divide 95 apples into 4 groups.
She uses long division and a model to solve the problem.

Step 1: Write the numbers like this:

the number of groups ⟶ 4)95 ⟵ the number of objects
to divide into groups

$95 = 9$ tens $+ 5$ ones

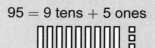

1. Fill in the blanks for the division statement.

a) 2)53

_____ groups

_____ tens

_____ ones

b) 5)71

_____ groups

_____ tens

_____ ones

c) 4)97

_____ groups

_____ tens

_____ ones

d) 5)88

_____ groups

_____ tens

_____ ones

Step 2: How many tens can be put in each group?

2 tens in each group ⟶ **2**

4 groups ⟶ 4)9 5

2. For each division problem, write how many groups have been made and how many
tens are in each group.

a) 4)5 5

_____ groups

_____ ten in
each group

b) 5)9 7

_____ groups

_____ ten in
each group

c) 3)7 6

_____ groups

_____ tens in
each group

d) 3)8 9

_____ groups

_____ tens in
each group

3. How many tens can be put in each group?

a) 4)8 7 with 2 on top

b) 3)9 4

c) 6)7 4

d) 2)9 8

e) 2)8 5

f) 3)6 7

g) 8)9 1

h) 3)8 2

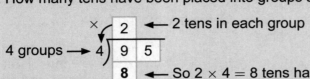

$2 \times 4 = 8$

×
2 ← 2 tens in each group

4 groups → 4) 9 5

8 ← So $2 \times 4 = 8$ tens have been placed

4. Multiply to decide how many tens have been placed.

a)
×
2
3) 8 7
6

b)
2
4) 9 9

c)
3
2) 7 9

d)
4
2) 8 9

5. Multiply to decide how many tens have been placed. Then answer the questions.

a)
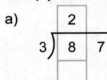
2
3) 8 7

How many groups? _____

How many tens? _____

How many tens in each group? _____

How many tens placed altogether? _____

b)
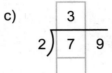
2
4) 9 6

How many groups? _____

How many tens? _____

How many tens in each group? _____

How many tens placed altogether? _____

6. Skip count to find out how many tens can be placed in each group. Then multiply to find out how many tens have been placed.

a)
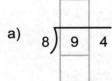
8) 9 4

b)
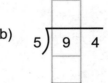
5) 9 4

c)
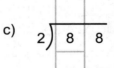
2) 8 8

d)
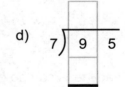
7) 9 5

e)
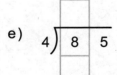
4) 8 5

f)
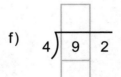
4) 9 2

g)
5) 6 3

h)
2) 9 8

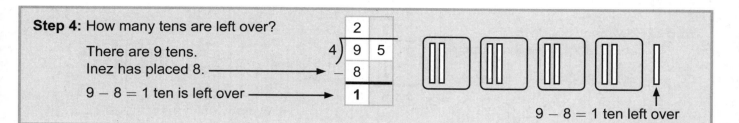

Step 4: How many tens are left over?

There are 9 tens.
Inez has placed 8.

$9 - 8 = 1$ ten is left over

$9 - 8 = 1$ ten left over

7. Carry out the first four steps of long division.

a)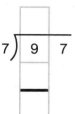

b)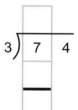

c)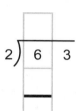

d)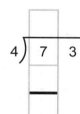

e)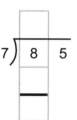

f)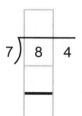

g)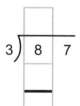

h)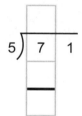

Step 5: There are 1 ten and 5 ones left over.
So there are 15 ones left over.

Write 5 beside the 1 to show this.

There are 15 ones still to place

8. Carry out the first five steps of long division.

a)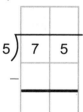

b)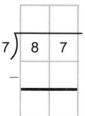

c)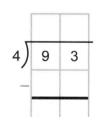

d)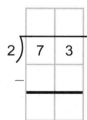

e)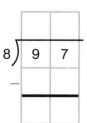

f)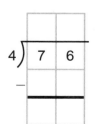

g)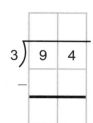

h)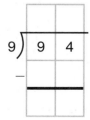

Step 6: How many of the 15 ones can be placed in each group?

Divide to find out.

 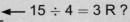 15 ÷ 4 = 3 R ?

   ?

How many ones are left over? _____

9. Carry out the first six steps of long division.

a)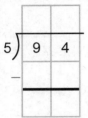

b)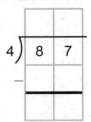

c)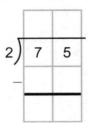

d)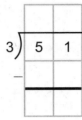

e)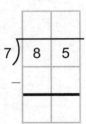

f)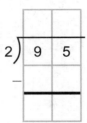

g)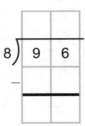

h)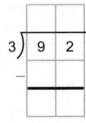

Step 7: How many ones are left over?

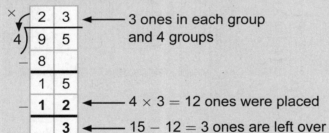 ← 3 ones in each group and 4 groups

   left over

← 4 × 3 = 12 ones were placed

← 15 − 12 = 3 ones are left over   **95 ÷ 4 = 23 with 3 left over**

10. Carry out all seven steps of long division.

a)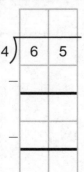

b)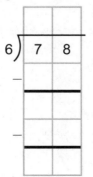

c)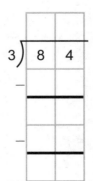

d)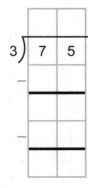

11. a) How many weeks are there in 84 days?

b) A boat can hold 4 children. How many boats will 72 children need?

36. Concepts in Multiplication and Division

1. Tom needs new tires for his car. Each tire costs $263. How much do all 4 tires cost?

2. Jennifer plants 84 lilies in 4 flower beds. How many lilies are in each flower bed?

3. A square park has a perimeter of 680 m. How long is each side of the park?

4. Jerry paid $276 for 6 sweaters. How much did each sweater cost?

5. Each side of a square field is 874 m long. What is the perimeter of the field?

6. A pentagon with equal sides has a perimeter of 325 cm. How long is each side?

7. A queen ant can lay one egg every ten seconds. How many eggs can she lay in ...

   a) 1 minute?   b) 2 minutes?   c) an hour?

8. 92 kids attend a play on 4 buses. There are an equal number of kids on each bus.

   a) How many kids are on each bus?

   b) A ticket for the play costs $6. How much will it cost for one busload of kids to attend the play?

9. Find two different ways to share 14 apples in equal groups so there are 2 apples left over.

10. Find three numbers that give the same remainder when divided by 3.

11. A robin lays at *least* 3 eggs and *no more* than 6 eggs.

   a) What is the least number of eggs 3 robins' nests would hold (if there were eggs laid in each nest)?

   b) What is the greatest number of eggs 3 robins' nests would hold?

   c) Three robins' nests contain 13 eggs. Draw a picture to show 2 ways the eggs could be shared among the nests.

37. Mental Math

1. Find the missing number in the multiplication. Then divide.

a) 300 × _____ = 3,000

so 3,000 ÷ 300 = _____

b) 40 × _____ = 4,000

so 4,000 ÷ 40 = _____

c) 20 × _____ = 20,000

so 20,000 ÷ 20 = _____

d) 600 × _____ = 60,000

so 60,000 ÷ 600 = _____

2. Divide mentally.

a) 9,000 ÷ 900

= _____

b) 6,000 ÷ 60

= _____

c) 80,000 ÷ 80

= _____

d) 70,000 ÷ 700

= _____

BONUS ▶ 80,000,000 ÷ 800 = _____

To find 86 ÷ 2, divide the tens and ones separately.

86 ÷ 2   =   80 ÷ 2   +   6 ÷ 2

43   =   40   +   3

3. Divide one place value at a time.

a) 64 ÷ 2 = (60 ÷ 2) + (4 ÷ 2)

= __30__ + __2__

= __32__

b) 69 ÷ 3 = (60 ÷ 3) + (9 ÷ 3)

= _____ + _____

= _____

c) 86 ÷ 2 = (80 ÷ 2) + (6 ÷ 2)

= _____ + _____

= _____

d) 96 ÷ 3 = (_____ ÷ 3) + (_____ ÷ 3)

= _____ + _____

= _____

BONUS ▶ 824 ÷ 2 = (800 ÷ 2) + (20 ÷ 2) + (4 ÷ 2)

4. Check your answer to Question 3 a) and b) by multiplication.

a)
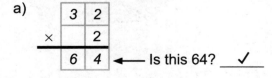
◄— Is this 64? ✓

b)
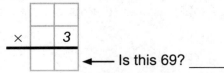
◄— Is this 69? _____

38. Mental Math (Advanced)

A rectangle with 4 squares down and 6 squares across has 24 squares in total.

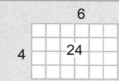

$4 \times 6 = 24$ so $24 \div 4 = 6$

1. How many squares across is the rectangle?

a) 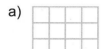 $12 \div 3 =$ _____

b)  $15 \div 3 =$ _____

2. Draw the rectangle to make the total number of squares. How many squares across do you need?

a)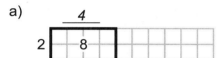

b)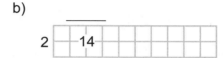

3. Decide how many squares across you need to make the rectangle. Then write the division equation.

a)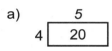

$\underline{\ \ 20 \div 4 = 5\ \ }$

b)
4 | 200

_____

c)
4 | 2,000

_____

d)
4 | 20,000

_____

Tara finds $36 \div 2$ by splitting 36 into tens and ones.

$36 = 30 + 6$ so

$36 \div 2 = 15 + 3 = 18$

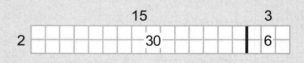

---

4. Use Tara's method to divide.

a) $92 \div 2$

$\underline{\ \ 45\ \ } + \underline{\ \ 1\ \ }$

| 90 | 2 |

2 |

$92 \div 2 = \underline{\ \ 46\ \ }$

b) $56 \div 2$

_____ + _____

| 50 | 6 |

2 |

$56 \div 2 =$ _____

c) $62 \div 2$

_____ + _____

2 |

$62 \div 2 =$ _____

d) $74 \div 2$

_____ + _____

2 |

$74 \div 2 =$ _____

Ron uses Tara's method to divide 78 ÷ 2, but...

... he chooses the tens and ones so that the **number of tens** is a multiple of the **number that he is dividing by**.

He uses the largest number of tens he can.

78 = 7 tens + 8 ones

= **6** tens + 18 ones

6 is a multiple of **2**

$$\begin{array}{c} 30 \quad + \quad 9 \\ 2\ \boxed{\begin{array}{c|c} 60 & 18 \end{array}} \end{array}$$

So 78 ÷ 2 = 39

5. Use Ron's method to divide.

a) 94 ÷ 2

94 = 9 tens + 4 ones

= 8 tens + _____ ones

8 is a multiple of 2

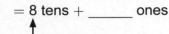
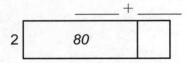

94 ÷ 2 = _____

b) 84 ÷ 3

84 = 8 tens + 4 ones

= 6 tens + _____ ones

6 is a multiple of 3

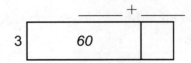

84 ÷ 3 = _____

c) 58 ÷ 2

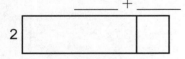

58 ÷ 2 = _____

d) 51 ÷ 3

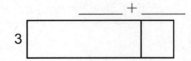

51 ÷ 3 = _____

e) 72 ÷ 3

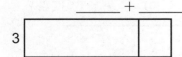

72 ÷ 3 = _____

f) 96 ÷ 4

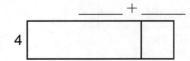

96 ÷ 4 = _____

6. A rectangular patio floor is covered with 84 tiles in 6 rows. How many tiles are in each row?

So there are _____ tiles in each row.

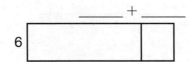

39. Interpreting Remainders

REMINDER ▶	dividend divisor quotient remainder
	35 ÷ 8 = 4 R 3

1. Circle the quotient. Underline the remainder.

   a) 42 ÷ 8 = 5 R 2   b) 27 ÷ 4 = 6 R 3   c) 31 ÷ 9 = 3 R 4   d) 15 ÷ 2 = 7 R 1

Sometimes the answer to a division problem is the quotient without the remainder.
Example: Jiba has $35. How many $8 T-shirts can she buy?

Solution: Skip count until the T-shirts cost too much money.

   $8 $16 $24 $32 $40 ◄—— This is too much money.

Then write the division: 35 ÷ 8 = 4 R 3. She can't buy part of a fifth T-shirt, so ignore the remainder.
The answer is the quotient: she can buy 4 T-shirts.

---

2. Jordan has $28. How many $5 movie tickets can he buy?

   a) Skip count by $5 until the movie tickets cost too much money.

   __$5__   __$10__   __$15__   _____   _____   _____   _____

   b) 28 ÷ 5 = _____ R _____

   c) How many tickets can Jordan buy? _____

   What part of the division equation is your answer? _____

3. Write a division statement. Then answer the question.

   a) Ahmed has $50. How many $12 T-shirts can he buy?

   50 ÷ 12 = _____ R _____ , so he can buy _____ T-shirts.

   b) Nancy has $82. How many $6 books can she buy?

   _____ ÷ _____ = _____ R _____ , so she can buy _____ books.

4. Nina has 20 tickets for rides at an amusement park. Each ride takes 3 tickets.
How many rides can she go on?

Sometimes the answer to a division problem is one more than the quotient.

Example: Each can holds 3 tennis balls. A tennis instructor needs 25 tennis balls.
How many cans does the instructor need to buy?

Solution: Draw 3 tennis balls in each can, until you have 25 tennis balls.

$25 \div 3 = 8$ R 1, so 8 cans are completely filled. You need one more can for the last ball.
So the instructor needs to buy 9 cans altogether.

5. Each can holds 3 tennis balls. A tennis instructor needs 14 tennis balls.

a) Draw 3 dots in each can until you have 14 dots. Then write the division equation.

$14 \div 3 = $ _____ R _____

b) How many cans are completely full? _____

c) How many cans does the instructor need to buy? _____

6. Ping needs to move 10 boxes. On each trip she can carry 4 boxes.
How many trips will she need to make?

_____ $\div$ _____ = _____ R _____ , so Ping needs to make _____ trips.

7. Write the division statement. Interpret the remainder to answer the question.

a) 82 people are going on a bus trip for school. Each bus holds 30 people.
How many buses are needed?

b) Ian has $82. Each sweater costs $30. How many sweaters can he buy?

c) Joni needs to raise $85. She sells pens for $3 each. How many pens does
she need to sell?

d) Nomi has 21 kg of salt. She sells it in 2 kg bags. How many bags can she sell?

e) 10 people are going on a canoe trip. Each canoe can hold 3 people.
How many canoes do they need?

f) Siru wants to place her stamps in an album. Each page holds 9 stamps.
How many pages will she need for 95 stamps?

JUMP Math Accumula

40. Interpreting Remainders (Advanced)

Sometimes the answer to a division problem is the remainder.

Example: Lee has 19 candies. He makes gift bags of 5 each, and he eats the leftover candies.
How many candies will he eat?

Solution: $19 \div 5 = 3$ R 4, so Lee makes 3 gift bags and eats 4 candies.

1. Write the division equation and circle the answer to each question.

   a) Juan has 15 apples. He makes gift bags of 4 each and keeps
      the leftover apples for himself. How many apples did he keep? _____ $\div$ _____ = _____ R _____

   b) Serena has 22 apples. She sells as many as she can in baskets
      of 4. How many apples does she have to sell separately? _____ $\div$ _____ = _____ R _____

   c) A store sells broccoli in packs of 4 stalks. They have 59 stalks.

      i) How many packs of broccoli can the store sell? _____ $\div$ _____ = _____ R _____

      ii) How many stalks of broccoli do they have to sell separately? _____ $\div$ _____ = _____ R _____

2. Write the division equation. Then answer the question.

   a) 26 people are going on a car trip. Each car holds 6 people.   ___$26 \div 6 = 4$ R 2___

      How many cars will they need? __5__

   b) A store has 800 pencils and sells them in packs of 9.   _____

      How many packs can they sell? _____

   c) A project requires 25 hours of work. Each volunteer can
      do 4 hours of work.   _____

      How many volunteers are needed? _____

   d) Bilal has $25. Baseballs cost $4.   _____

      How many baseballs can he buy? _____

      How much money will he have left over? _____

   e) Esther needs to move 23 boxes. On each trip she can
      carry 3 boxes. She carries as many as she can each time.   _____

      How many trips does she make? _____

      How many boxes does she carry on her last trip? _____

41. Naming Fractions

The area is cut into 4 equal parts.

3 parts out of 4 are shaded.

$\frac{3}{4}$ of the area is shaded.

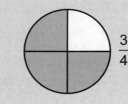

The **numerator** (3) tells you three parts are shaded.

$\frac{3}{4}$

The **denominator** (4) tells you how many equal parts are in a whole.

1. Name the fraction shown by the shaded part of each image.

a)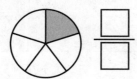

b)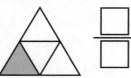

c)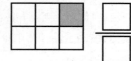

d)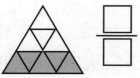

e)

f)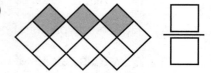

2. Shade the fractions named.

a) $\frac{1}{6}$

b) $\frac{1}{5}$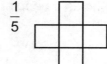

c) $\frac{1}{9}$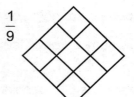

d) $\frac{3}{6}$

e) $\frac{2}{5}$

f) $\frac{5}{9}$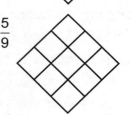

3. Use one of the following words to describe each square in the figures below.

half   **third**   **fourth**   **fifth**   **sixth**   **seventh**   **eighth**   **ninth**

a)

b)

c)

_____

_____

_____

42. Comparing Fractions (Introduction)

1. Which strip has more shaded? Circle its fraction.

a) 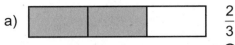 $\frac{2}{3}$

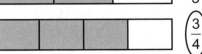 $\left(\frac{3}{4}\right)$

b) 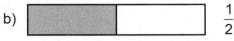 $\frac{1}{2}$

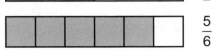 $\frac{5}{6}$

c)  $\frac{2}{3}$

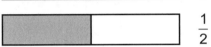 $\frac{1}{2}$

d) 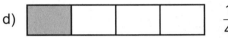 $\frac{1}{4}$

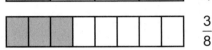 $\frac{3}{8}$

e) 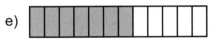 $\frac{7}{12}$

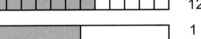 $\frac{1}{2}$

f) 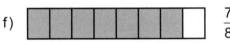 $\frac{7}{8}$

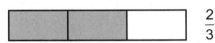 $\frac{2}{3}$

$\frac{1}{2}$ is **greater than** $\frac{1}{3}$ because more is shaded.

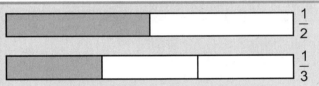 $\frac{1}{2}$

$\frac{1}{3}$

2. Shade the amounts. Circle the greater fraction.

a)  $\frac{2}{3}$

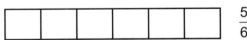 $\frac{5}{6}$

b) 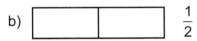 $\frac{1}{2}$

 $\frac{3}{8}$

c) 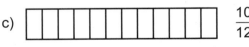 $\frac{10}{12}$

$\frac{3}{4}$

d) $\frac{1}{4}$

$\frac{1}{3}$

"5 is greater than 3" is written $5 > 3$.   "3 is less than 5" is written $3 < 5$.

3. Write your answers to Question 2 using $<$ or $>$.

a) $\frac{2}{3} \square \frac{5}{6}$ b) $\frac{1}{2} \square \frac{3}{8}$ c) $\frac{10}{12} \square \frac{3}{4}$ d) $\frac{1}{4} \square \frac{1}{3}$

One third **equals** two sixths because
the same amount is shaded.

$\frac{1}{3}$ and $\frac{2}{6}$ are called **equivalent** fractions.

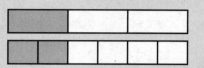

4. Complete the equivalent fractions.

a) 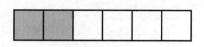 $\frac{1}{2} = \frac{}{4}$

b) 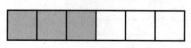 $\frac{1}{2} = \frac{}{6}$

c) $\frac{1}{3} = \frac{}{6}$

d) $\frac{2}{3} = \frac{}{6}$

e) $\frac{2}{2} = \frac{}{10}$

f) $\frac{4}{10} = \frac{}{5}$

5. Use the picture to find the equivalent fractions.

a)

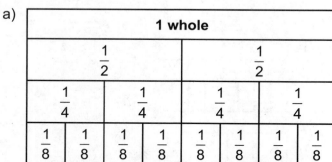

1 whole							
$\frac{1}{2}$				$\frac{1}{2}$			
$\frac{1}{4}$		$\frac{1}{4}$		$\frac{1}{4}$		$\frac{1}{4}$	
$\frac{1}{8}$	$\frac{1}{8}$	$\frac{1}{8}$	$\frac{1}{8}$	$\frac{1}{8}$	$\frac{1}{8}$	$\frac{1}{8}$	$\frac{1}{8}$

$\frac{1}{4} = \frac{}{8}$ $\frac{1}{2} = \frac{}{8}$

$\frac{6}{8} = \frac{}{4}$ $\frac{2}{4} = \frac{}{2}$

b)

1 whole									
$\frac{1}{5}$		$\frac{1}{5}$		$\frac{1}{5}$		$\frac{1}{5}$		$\frac{1}{5}$	
$\frac{1}{10}$	$\frac{1}{10}$	$\frac{1}{10}$	$\frac{1}{10}$	$\frac{1}{10}$	$\frac{1}{10}$	$\frac{1}{10}$	$\frac{1}{10}$	$\frac{1}{10}$	$\frac{1}{10}$

$\frac{1}{5} = \frac{}{10}$ $\frac{6}{10} = \frac{}{5}$

$\frac{4}{5} = \frac{}{10}$ $\frac{5}{5} = \frac{}{10}$

43. Equal Parts and Models of Fractions

1. Use a centimeter ruler to divide the line into equal parts. The first one is started for you.

   a) 5 equal parts

   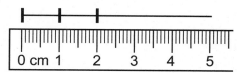

   b) 8 equal parts

   _____

   c) 6 equal parts

   _____

2. Using a ruler, join the marks to divide the box into equal parts.

   a) 4 equal parts

   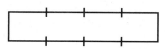

   b) 5 equal parts

3. Mark the box in centimeters. Then divide the box into equal parts.

   a) 3 equal parts

   b) 6 equal parts

4. Using a ruler, find what fraction of the box is shaded.

   a)

   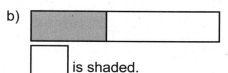

   is shaded.

   b)

   is shaded.

5. Using a ruler, complete the figure to make a whole.

   a) $\dfrac{1}{2}$

   b) $\dfrac{2}{3}$

6. Sketch a rectangle cut in halves. Then cut it in fourths.

7. You have $\dfrac{3}{8}$ of a pie.

   a) What does the bottom (denominator) of the fraction tell you?

   b) What does the top (numerator) of the fraction tell you?

8. Explain why each picture does (or does not) show $\dfrac{1}{4}$.

   a)   b)   c)   d)

44. NF4-4 Fractions on Number Lines

We can use number lines instead of fraction strips to show fractions.

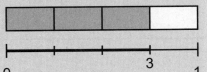 $\dfrac{3}{4}$ of the strip is shaded.

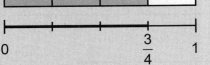 $\dfrac{3}{4}$ of the number line from 0 to 1 is shaded.

1. Find what fraction of the number line from 0 to 1 is shaded.

a)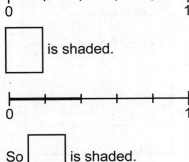

is shaded.

So ☐ is shaded.

b)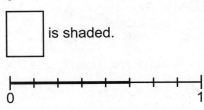

is shaded.

So ☐ is shaded.

To find $\dfrac{3}{4}$ on a number line, divide the number line from 0 to 1 into **4** equal parts.
Then start at 0 and take **3** parts.

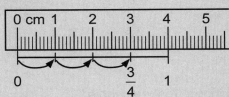

2. Use a ruler to divide the number line from 0 to 1 into equal parts, and then mark the fraction.

a) 3 equal parts and mark $\dfrac{1}{3}$

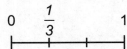

b) 5 equal parts and mark $\dfrac{2}{5}$

```
0                    1
├────────────────────┤
```

c) 6 equal parts and mark $\dfrac{3}{6}$

```
0                              1
├──────────────────────────────┤
```

d) 8 equal parts and mark $\dfrac{6}{8}$

```
0                              1
├──────────────────────────────┤
```

3. Pamela marks $\frac{3}{4}$ on the number line. John marks $\frac{2}{3}$ on the same number line.

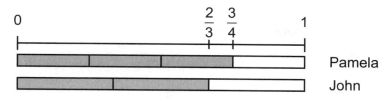

Which fraction is bigger? ☐

You can use number lines to compare fractions.

$\frac{3}{4}$ is greater than $\frac{2}{4}$ because it is farther to the right: $\frac{3}{4} > \frac{2}{4}$.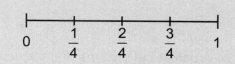

4. Anna placed fractions with different denominators on the same number line.

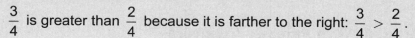

a) Write < (less than) or > (greater than).

i) $\frac{1}{8}$ ☐ $\frac{1}{2}$

ii) $\frac{3}{4}$ ☐ $\frac{1}{3}$

iii) $\frac{5}{6}$ ☐ $\frac{3}{4}$

b) Circle these fractions on the number line above. Then write them from greatest to least.

$\frac{1}{2}, \frac{5}{6}, \frac{1}{3}$ ☐ > ☐ > ☐

Two fractions are equivalent if they mark the same place on a number line from 0 to 1.

5. Use the number lines to find equivalent fractions.

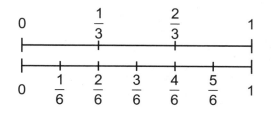

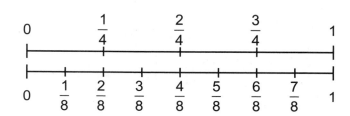

a) $\frac{1}{3} = \frac{}{6}$

b) $\frac{2}{3} = \frac{}{6}$

c) $\frac{1}{4} = \frac{}{8}$

d) $\frac{3}{4} = \frac{}{8}$

45. More Comparing Fractions

REMINDER ▶ $\dfrac{3}{8}$ ◀——— The numerator tells you how many parts are counted.
◀——— The denominator tells you how many equal parts are in one whole.

1. a) Write the numerators of the shaded fractions.

$\overline{4}$ $\overline{4}$ $\overline{4}$

b) Look at the pictures and fractions in part a). Write "increases," "decreases," or "stays the same."

i) The numerator _____.

ii) The denominator _____.

iii) The fraction shaded _____.

Same number of parts in one whole   and   *more parts shaded*   ——▶   *more shaded*

same denominator   and   *larger numerator*   ——▶   *greater fraction*

$\dfrac{3}{5} > \dfrac{2}{5}$ because 3 fifths is more than 2 fifths.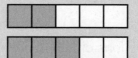

---

2. Circle the greater fraction in each pair.

a) $\dfrac{3}{8}$ or $\dfrac{6}{8}$ b) $\dfrac{7}{12}$ or $\dfrac{4}{12}$ c) $\dfrac{5}{10}$ or $\dfrac{2}{10}$ BONUS ▶ $\dfrac{74}{85}$ or $\dfrac{69}{85}$

3. Write the fractions in order from least to greatest.

a) $\dfrac{2}{3}, \dfrac{1}{3}, \dfrac{3}{3}$

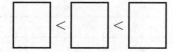

b) $\dfrac{2}{10}, \dfrac{1}{10}, \dfrac{7}{10}, \dfrac{9}{10}$

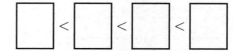

4. Write a fraction between $\dfrac{3}{8}$ and $\dfrac{7}{8}$.

5. a) What fraction of a cup is in the container?

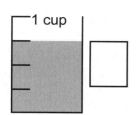   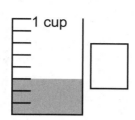   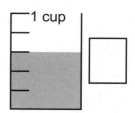

b) Place the fractions from part a) in order from least to greatest.

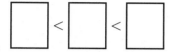

c) Write "bigger" or "smaller":

As the denominator (bottom) of the fraction gets bigger, each part gets _____.

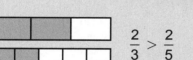

Same number of parts shaded   and   bigger parts   ⟶   more shaded

same numerator   and   smaller denominator   ⟶   greater fraction

$$\frac{2}{3} > \frac{2}{5}$$

6. Circle the greater fraction in each pair.

a) $\frac{1}{5}$ or $\frac{1}{6}$ b) $\frac{3}{10}$ or $\frac{3}{8}$ c) $\frac{5}{12}$ or $\frac{5}{10}$ **BONUS ▶** $\frac{93}{100}$ or $\frac{93}{1,000}$

7. Write the fractions in order from least to greatest.

a) $\frac{1}{5}, \frac{1}{2}, \frac{1}{4}$

b) $\frac{4}{6}, \frac{4}{8}, \frac{4}{10}, \frac{4}{9}$

8. Write a fraction between $\frac{2}{9}$ and $\frac{2}{3}$.

9. a) Two fractions have the same *numerators* (tops) but different *denominators* (bottoms). How can you tell which fraction is greater?

b) Two fractions have the same *denominators* (bottoms) but different *numerators* (tops). How can you tell which fraction is greater?

46. Equivalent Fractions and Multiplication

1. How many times as many parts?

a) 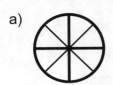 has _____ times as many parts as

b) has _____ times as many parts as

c) has _____ times as many parts as

d) has _____ times as many parts as

2. Fill in the blanks.

a) A has _____ times as many parts as B.

   A has _____ times as many shaded parts as B.

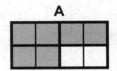

b) A has _____ times as many parts as B.

   A has _____ times as many shaded parts as B.

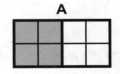 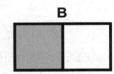

c) A has _____ times as many parts as B.

   A has _____ times as many shaded parts as B.

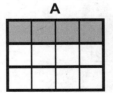 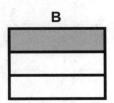

d) A has _____ times as many parts as B.

   A has _____ times as many shaded parts as B.

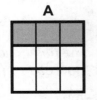 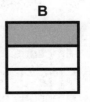

3. The picture shows two equivalent fractions. Fill in the blanks.

a) 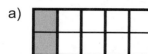 $\frac{1}{5}$ and $\frac{2}{10}$

2 is _____ times as much as 1.

10 is _____ times as much as 5.

b)  $\frac{4}{5}$ and $\frac{12}{15}$

12 is _____ times as much as 4.

15 is _____ times as much as 5.

c) 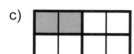 $\frac{1}{4}$ and $\frac{2}{8}$

2 is _____ times as much as 1.

8 is _____ times as much as 4.

d) 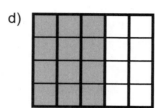 $\frac{3}{5}$ and $\frac{12}{20}$

12 is _____ times as much as 3.

20 is _____ times as much as 5.

4. Write an equivalent fraction for the picture. Then write how many times as much the new numerator and denominator are.

a)  $\frac{3}{4} = \boxed{\frac{9}{12}}$

____3___ times as much

b) 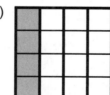 $\frac{1}{4} = \boxed{}$

_____ times as much

c) 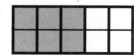 $\frac{3}{5} = \boxed{}$

_____ times as much

BONUS ▶

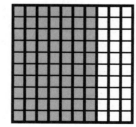 $\frac{7}{10} = \boxed{}$

_____ times as much

To get an equivalent fraction, multiply the numerator and denominator by the same number.

Example:　Picture A 　$\dfrac{3}{4} \xrightarrow[\times 2]{\times 2} \dfrac{6}{8}$　Picture B

Picture B has twice as many **parts** as Picture A.
Picture B has twice as many **shaded parts** as Picture A.

5. Draw lines to cut the pies into more equal pieces. Then fill in the numerators of the equivalent fractions.

a)

4 pieces　　6 pieces　　8 pieces

$$\frac{1}{2} = \frac{}{4} = \frac{}{6} = \frac{}{8}$$

b)

6 pieces　　9 pieces　　12 pieces

$$\frac{1}{3} = \frac{}{6} = \frac{}{9} = \frac{}{12}$$

6. Cut each pie into more pieces. Then fill in the missing numbers.

a) 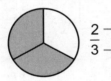　$\dfrac{2}{3} \xrightarrow[\times 2]{\times 2} \dfrac{}{6}$

b) $\dfrac{3}{4} \xrightarrow[\times 2]{\times 2} \dfrac{}{8}$

c) $\dfrac{2}{3} \xrightarrow[\times]{\times} \dfrac{}{9}$

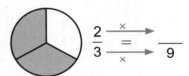

This number tells you how many pieces to cut each slice into.

7. Use multiplication to find the equivalent fraction.

a) $\dfrac{1 \times 2}{3 \times 2} = \dfrac{}{6}$　　　b) $\dfrac{1 \times}{2 \times} = \dfrac{}{10}$　　　c) $\dfrac{2}{5} = \dfrac{}{10}$

d) $\dfrac{3}{4} = \dfrac{}{8}$　　　e) $\dfrac{1}{4} = \dfrac{}{12}$　　　f) $\dfrac{4}{5} = \dfrac{}{15}$

g) $\dfrac{5}{6} = \dfrac{}{12}$　　　h) $\dfrac{3}{10} = \dfrac{}{100}$　　　i) $\dfrac{5}{9} = \dfrac{}{72}$

8. Write five fractions equivalent to $\dfrac{7}{10}$.

$$\frac{7}{10} = \boxed{} = \boxed{} = \boxed{} = \boxed{} = \boxed{}$$

　　　JUMP Math Accumula

47. Comparing Fractions Using Equivalent Fractions

1. Draw lines to cut the pies into more equal pieces. Then fill in the numerators of the equivalent fractions.

a)

$$\frac{2}{3} = \frac{}{6} = \frac{}{9} = \frac{}{12} = \frac{}{15}$$

b)

$$\frac{3}{5} = \frac{}{10} = \frac{}{15} = \frac{}{20} = \frac{}{25}$$

2. a) Write two fractions with the same denominator. Hint: Use your answers from Question 1.

$$\frac{2}{3} = \boxed{} \text{ and } \frac{3}{5} = \boxed{}$$

b) Which of the two fractions is greater, $\frac{2}{3}$ or $\frac{3}{5}$? _____

How do you know? _____

_____

3. Rewrite the fractions so that they have the same denominator. Then circle the larger fraction.

a) $\frac{1}{3} = \frac{}{15}$ and $\frac{2}{5} = \frac{}{15}$

b) $\frac{3}{8} = \frac{}{24}$ and $\frac{1}{3} = \frac{}{24}$

4. a) Write an equivalent fraction with denominator 12.

i) $\frac{2}{3} = \frac{}{12}$ ii) $\frac{5}{6} = \frac{}{12}$ iii) $\frac{3}{4} = \frac{}{12}$ iv) $\frac{1}{2} = \frac{}{12}$

b) Write the fractions from part a) in order from least to greatest.

 < < <

5. Draw lines to cut the left-hand pie into the same number of equal pieces as the right-hand pie. Complete the equivalent fraction. Then circle the greater fraction.

a)

$$\frac{1}{2} = \frac{}{4} \qquad \frac{1}{4}$$

b)

$$\frac{2}{3} = \frac{}{6} \qquad \frac{5}{6}$$

6. Turn the fraction on the left into an equivalent fraction with the same denominator as the fraction on the right. Then write < (less than) or > (greater than) to show which fraction is greater.

a) $\dfrac{1 \times 3}{2 \times 3} = \dfrac{3}{6} \ \square \ \dfrac{4}{6}$

b) $\dfrac{1 \times}{2 \times} = \dfrac{}{8} \ \square \ \dfrac{5}{8}$

c) $\dfrac{1}{2} = \dfrac{}{} \ \square \ \dfrac{3}{4}$

d) $\dfrac{1}{3} = \dfrac{}{} \ \square \ \dfrac{2}{9}$

e) $\dfrac{1}{5} = \dfrac{}{} \ \square \ \dfrac{7}{10}$

f) $\dfrac{1}{4} = \dfrac{}{} \ \square \ \dfrac{3}{16}$

Pedro wants to turn $\dfrac{1}{3}$ and $\dfrac{2}{5}$ into fractions with the same denominator.

He multiplies the denominators together: $3 \times 5 = 5 \times 3$.

$$\dfrac{5 \times 1}{5 \times 3} \text{ and } \dfrac{2 \times 3}{5 \times 3}$$

$$= \dfrac{5}{15} \qquad = \dfrac{6}{15} \qquad\qquad \dfrac{5}{15} < \dfrac{6}{15}, \text{ so } \dfrac{1}{3} < \dfrac{2}{5}$$

---

7. Turn the fractions into fractions with the same denominator. Then compare the fractions. Show your answer using < or >.

a) $\dfrac{7 \times 3}{7 \times 4} \quad \dfrac{5 \times 4}{7 \times 4}$

b) $\dfrac{\times 1}{\times 2} \quad \dfrac{2 \times}{3 \times}$

c) $\dfrac{\times 1}{\times 2} \quad \dfrac{3 \times}{4 \times}$

d) $\dfrac{\times 2}{\times 3} \quad \dfrac{5 \times}{8 \times}$

$= \dfrac{}{28} \quad = \dfrac{}{28}$

$= \dfrac{}{} \quad = \dfrac{}{}$

$= \dfrac{}{} \quad = \dfrac{}{}$

$= \dfrac{}{} \quad = \dfrac{}{}$

so $\dfrac{3}{4} \ \square \ \dfrac{5}{7}$

so $\dfrac{1}{2} \ \square \ \dfrac{2}{3}$

so $\dfrac{1}{2} \ \square \ \dfrac{3}{4}$

so $\dfrac{2}{3} \ \square \ \dfrac{5}{8}$

8. Draw a picture to justify your answer to Question 7 c).

---

48. Adding Fractions

1. Tom took one piece from each pizza. Combine the pieces onto one plate.
   What fraction of a pizza did he take?

a)

$$\frac{1}{4} \quad + \quad \frac{1}{4} \quad = \quad \frac{2}{4}$$

b)

$$\frac{1}{3} \quad + \quad \frac{1}{3} \quad =$$

c)

$$\frac{1}{8} \quad + \quad \frac{1}{8} \quad + \quad \frac{1}{8} \quad + \quad \frac{1}{8} \quad + \quad \frac{1}{8} \quad =$$

Since $1 + 1 + 1 = 3$, so 1 fifth + 1 fifth + 1 fifth = 3 fifths.
$$\frac{1}{5} \quad + \quad \frac{1}{5} \quad + \quad \frac{1}{5} \quad = \quad \frac{3}{5}$$

2. Add. Then write the addition equation.

a) 1 fifth + 1 fifth = ___2___ fifths

$$\frac{1}{5} \quad + \quad \frac{1}{5} \quad = \quad \frac{2}{5}$$

b) 1 eighth + 1 eighth = _____ eighths

c) 1 third + 1 third + 1 third + 1 third = _____ thirds

3. Add.

a) $\frac{1}{3} + \frac{1}{3} =$

b) $\frac{1}{5} + \frac{1}{5} + \frac{1}{5} + \frac{1}{5} + \frac{1}{5} + \frac{1}{5} =$

c) $\frac{1}{8} + \frac{1}{8} + \frac{1}{8} + \frac{1}{8} + \frac{1}{8} + \frac{1}{8} + \frac{1}{8} =$

d) $\frac{1}{7} + \frac{1}{7} + \frac{1}{7} + \frac{1}{7} =$

4. Write the fraction as a sum of fractions with numerator 1.

a) $\frac{4}{5} =$

b) $\frac{3}{2} =$

49. Adding and Subtracting Fractions

1. Combine the pieces of pie onto one plate. Then write a fraction for the part you shaded.

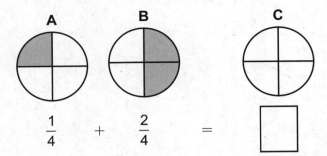

$$\frac{1}{4} \quad + \quad \frac{2}{4} \quad = \quad \boxed{}$$

2. Combine the liquid from the two cups. Then complete the addition equations.

a)
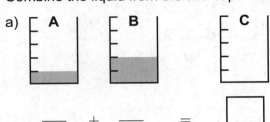

$$\frac{}{5} \quad + \quad \frac{}{5} \quad = \quad \boxed{}$$

b)
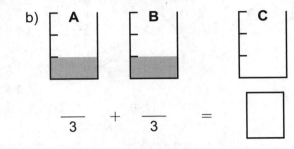

$$\frac{}{3} \quad + \quad \frac{}{3} \quad = \quad \boxed{}$$

3. Add.

a)
$$\frac{3}{8} \qquad + \qquad \frac{2}{8}$$

$$\frac{1}{8} + \frac{1}{8} + \frac{1}{8} \quad + \quad \frac{1}{8} + \frac{1}{8} = \boxed{\frac{5}{8}}$$

b)
$$\frac{2}{5} \qquad + \qquad \frac{4}{5}$$

$$\frac{1}{5} + \frac{1}{5} \quad + \quad \frac{1}{5} + \frac{1}{5} + \frac{1}{5} + \frac{1}{5} = \boxed{}$$

c)
$$\frac{2}{4} \qquad\qquad + \qquad\qquad \frac{5}{4}$$

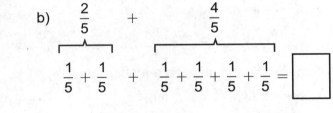

$$= \boxed{}$$

4. Write the addition equation.

a) $\boxed{}$ + $\boxed{}$ = $\boxed{}$

$$\frac{1}{3} + \frac{1}{3} \quad + \quad \frac{1}{3} + \frac{1}{3} + \frac{1}{3} + \frac{1}{3} + \frac{1}{3}$$

b) $\boxed{}$ + $\boxed{}$ = $\boxed{}$

$$\frac{1}{4} + \frac{1}{4} + \frac{1}{4} \quad + \quad \frac{1}{4} + \frac{1}{4} + \frac{1}{4}$$

5. Add the fractions.

a) $\dfrac{3}{5} + \dfrac{3}{5} =$ b) $\dfrac{2}{4} + \dfrac{1}{4} =$ c) $\dfrac{3}{7} + \dfrac{6}{7} =$ d) $\dfrac{5}{8} + \dfrac{2}{8} =$

6. Subtract by taking away the second amount.

a) $\dfrac{5}{4} - \dfrac{2}{4} = \boxed{\dfrac{3}{4}}$

$\dfrac{1}{4} + \dfrac{1}{4} + \dfrac{1}{4} + \boxed{\dfrac{1}{4} + \dfrac{1}{4}}$ ↗

b) $\dfrac{5}{8} - \dfrac{3}{8} = \boxed{}$

$\dfrac{1}{8} + \dfrac{1}{8} + \boxed{\dfrac{1}{8} + \dfrac{1}{8} + \dfrac{1}{8}}$ ↗

c) $\dfrac{7}{5} - \dfrac{4}{5} = \boxed{}$

$\dfrac{1}{5} + \dfrac{1}{5} + \dfrac{1}{5} + \dfrac{1}{5} + \dfrac{1}{5} + \dfrac{1}{5} + \dfrac{1}{5}$

d) $\dfrac{4}{3} - \dfrac{2}{3} = \boxed{}$

Break $\dfrac{4}{3}$ into thirds. Then take away $\dfrac{2}{3}$.

7. Subtract.

a) $\dfrac{2}{3} - \dfrac{1}{3} =$

b) $\dfrac{3}{5} - \dfrac{2}{5} =$

c) $\dfrac{6}{7} - \dfrac{3}{7} =$

d) $\dfrac{11}{5} - \dfrac{3}{5} =$

8. Mark ate $\dfrac{3}{10}$ of a pizza and Sarah ate $\dfrac{4}{10}$ of the pizza.

a) What fraction of the pizza did they eat altogether? $\boxed{}$

b) Write the equation that shows your answer to a).

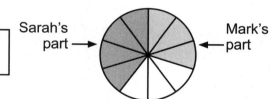

Sarah's part → ← Mark's part

_____

9. Pedro ate $\dfrac{2}{8}$ of a pie and Noreen ate $\dfrac{3}{8}$ of the pie.

a) Use the picture to show how much each person ate.

b) What fraction of the pie did they eat altogether?

c) Write the equation that shows your answer to b).

10. Katya ate $\dfrac{3}{5}$ of a pie. Roman ate the rest.

a) Use the picture to show how much each person ate.

b) Write an equation that shows how much Roman ate.

11. Angela adds $\dfrac{4}{10} + \dfrac{1}{10}$. She says her answer is equal to $\dfrac{1}{2}$. Is she right? Explain.

50. Improper Fractions and Mixed Numbers (Introduction)

Alan and his friends ate **9** quarter-sized pieces of pizza.

Altogether they ate $\frac{9}{4}$ pizzas.

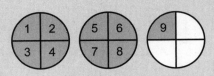

When the numerator of a fraction is larger than the denominator, the fraction represents **more than** one whole. Such fractions are called **improper fractions**.

1. Write an improper fraction for each picture.

   a)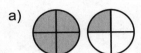

   b)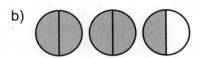

2. Shade one piece at a time until you have shaded the amount of pie given.

   a) $\frac{5}{2}$

   b) $\frac{7}{2}$

   c) $\frac{8}{3}$

   d) $\frac{13}{4}$

Alan and his friends ate two and one quarter pies (or $2\frac{1}{4}$ pies):

$2\frac{1}{4}$ is called a **mixed number** because it is a mixture of a whole number and a fraction.

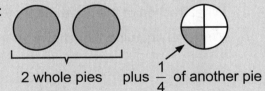

2 whole pies   plus $\frac{1}{4}$ of another pie

3. Write how many **whole** pies are shaded.

   a)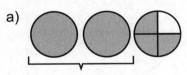

   __2__ whole pies

   b) _____ whole pies

   c)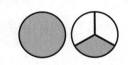

   _____ whole pie

4. Write the fraction as a mixed number.

   a)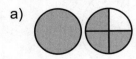

   _____

   b)

   _____

5. Shade the amount of pie given. There may be more pies in the picture than you need.

a) $2\frac{1}{2}$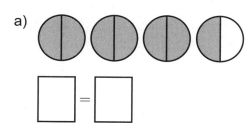

b) $3\frac{2}{3}$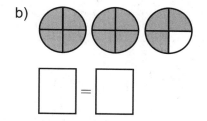

6. Write these fractions as mixed numbers and as improper fractions.

a)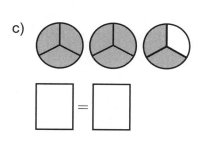

b)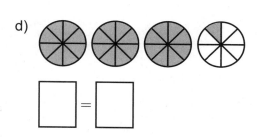

c)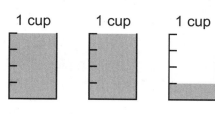

d)

7. Write a mixed number and an improper fraction for the number of cups.

1 cup   1 cup   1 cup

mixed number ☐   improper fraction ☐

8. Shade the amount of pie given. Then write an improper fraction for the amount of pie.

a) $2\frac{1}{2}$ 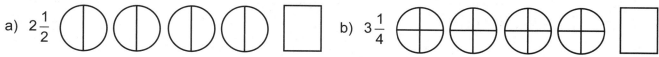 ☐   b) $3\frac{1}{4}$ ☐

9. Shade the amount of pie given. Then write a mixed number for the amount of pie.

a) $\frac{7}{3}$ 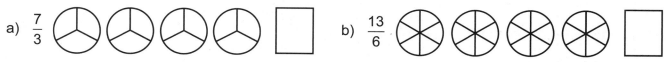 ☐   b) $\frac{13}{6}$ ☐

10. Sketch the pies. Then write an equivalent mixed number or improper fraction.

a) $2\frac{1}{2}$ pies   b) $\frac{9}{2}$ pies   c) $\frac{10}{4}$ pies   d) $3\frac{2}{3}$ pies

51. Improper Fractions and Mixed Numbers

How many quarter pieces are in $2\frac{1}{4}$ pies?

4 quarters

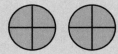

8 (= 2 × 4) quarters

8 quarters + 1 extra quarter = 9 quarters

So there are 9 quarter-sized pieces altogether.

1. Find the number of **halves** in each amount.

   a) 1 pie = _____ halves

   $1\frac{1}{2}$ pies = _____ halves

   b) 2 pies = _____ halves

   $2\frac{1}{2}$ pies = _____ halves

   c) 3 pies = _____ halves

   $3\frac{1}{2}$ pies = _____ halves

2. Find the number of **thirds** in each amount.

   a) 1 pie = _____ thirds

   $1\frac{1}{3}$ pies = _____ thirds

   b) 2 pies = _____ thirds

   $2\frac{2}{3}$ pies = _____ thirds

   c) 3 pies = _____ thirds

   $3\frac{1}{3}$ pies = _____ thirds

3. Find the number of **quarters** (or fourths) in each amount. Then write the mixed number as an improper fraction.

   a) $1\frac{1}{4}$ pies = 1 pie + $\frac{1}{4}$ pie

   $= \underline{\ \ 4\ \ }$ quarters

   $+ \underline{\ \ 1\ \ }$ quarter

   $= \underline{\ \ 5\ \ }$ quarters

   $= \dfrac{5}{4}$

   b) $2\frac{3}{4}$ pies = 2 pies + $\frac{3}{4}$ pies

   $= \underline{\quad}$ quarters

   $= \underline{\quad}$ quarters

   $= \underline{\quad}$ quarters

   $= \dfrac{\square}{\square}$

   c) $3\frac{2}{4}$ pies = 3 pies + $\frac{2}{4}$ pies

   $= \underline{\quad}$ quarters

   $= \underline{\quad}$ quarters

   $= \underline{\quad}$ quarters

   $= \dfrac{\square}{\square}$

4. Write the mixed number as an improper fraction.

   a) $3\frac{1}{4} =$

   b) $3\frac{4}{5} =$

   c) $5\frac{1}{2} =$

   d) $2\frac{1}{5} =$

   e) $5\frac{2}{3} =$

   f) $7\frac{3}{10} =$

5. Pens come in packs of 8. Dan used $1\frac{5}{8}$ packs. How many pens did he use? _____

6. Bottles come in packs of 6. How many bottles are in $2\frac{5}{6}$ packs? _____

7. Circle groups that equal 1. Then write the improper fraction as a mixed number.

a) $\dfrac{7}{3} = \boxed{\dfrac{1}{3} + \dfrac{1}{3} + \dfrac{1}{3}} + \boxed{\dfrac{1}{3} + \dfrac{1}{3} + \dfrac{1}{3}} + \dfrac{1}{3} = 2\dfrac{1}{3}$

b) $\dfrac{9}{2} = \boxed{\dfrac{1}{2} + \dfrac{1}{2}} + \boxed{\dfrac{1}{2} + \dfrac{1}{2}} + \boxed{\dfrac{1}{2} + \dfrac{1}{2}} + \boxed{\dfrac{1}{2} + \dfrac{1}{2}} + \dfrac{1}{2} =$

c) $\dfrac{11}{4} = \dfrac{1}{4} + \dfrac{1}{4} + \dfrac{1}{4} + \dfrac{1}{4} + \dfrac{1}{4} + \dfrac{1}{4} + \dfrac{1}{4} + \dfrac{1}{4} + \dfrac{1}{4} + \dfrac{1}{4} + \dfrac{1}{4} =$

d) $\dfrac{11}{3} = \dfrac{1}{3} + \dfrac{1}{3} + \dfrac{1}{3} + \dfrac{1}{3} + \dfrac{1}{3} + \dfrac{1}{3} + \dfrac{1}{3} + \dfrac{1}{3} + \dfrac{1}{3} + \dfrac{1}{3} + \dfrac{1}{3} =$

e) $\dfrac{12}{5} = \dfrac{1}{5} + \dfrac{1}{5} + \dfrac{1}{5} + \dfrac{1}{5} + \dfrac{1}{5} + \dfrac{1}{5} + \dfrac{1}{5} + \dfrac{1}{5} + \dfrac{1}{5} + \dfrac{1}{5} + \dfrac{1}{5} + \dfrac{1}{5} =$

How many wholes are in $\dfrac{9}{4}$? A whole is 4 quarters, so make groups of 4:

$$\dfrac{9}{4} = \boxed{\dfrac{1}{4} + \dfrac{1}{4} + \dfrac{1}{4} + \dfrac{1}{4}} + \boxed{\dfrac{1}{4} + \dfrac{1}{4} + \dfrac{1}{4} + \dfrac{1}{4}} + \dfrac{1}{4} = 2\dfrac{1}{4}$$

There are 2 groups of four quarters, and 1 quarter is left over. Since $9 \div 4 = 2$ R 1, then $\dfrac{9}{4} = 2\dfrac{1}{4}$.

---

8. Find the number of wholes in each amount by dividing.

a) $\dfrac{4}{2} = $ _____ wholes

b) $\dfrac{6}{2} = $ _____ wholes

c) $\dfrac{10}{2} = $ _____ wholes

9. Write the improper fraction as a mixed number by dividing.

a) $\dfrac{9}{2}$

$9 \div 2 = $ _____ R _____

So $\dfrac{9}{2} = \boxed{}$

b) $\dfrac{15}{4}$

$15 \div 4 = $ _____ R _____

So $\dfrac{15}{4} = \boxed{}$

c) $\dfrac{22}{5}$

$22 \div 5 = $ _____ R _____

So $\dfrac{22}{5} = \boxed{}$

d) $\dfrac{14}{5} =$

e) $\dfrac{68}{10} =$

f) $\dfrac{32}{8} =$

g) $\dfrac{30}{8} =$

h) $\dfrac{40}{7} =$

i) $\dfrac{28}{7} =$

52. Adding and Subtracting Mixed Numbers

1. How many halves are in each amount?

   a) $3\frac{1}{2} + 4\frac{1}{2}$ $(3 \times 2) + 1$

      $= \underline{\quad 7 \quad}$ halves $+ \underline{\quad 9 \quad}$ halves

      $= \underline{\quad 16 \quad}$ halves

   b) $5 + 1\frac{1}{2}$

      $= \underline{\qquad}$ halves $+ \underline{\qquad}$ halves

      $= \underline{\qquad}$ halves

   c) $6\frac{1}{2} - 2$

      $= \underline{\qquad}$ halves $- \underline{\qquad}$ halves

      $= \underline{\qquad}$ halves

   d) $4 - 1\frac{1}{2}$

      $= \underline{\qquad}$ halves $- \underline{\qquad}$ halves

      $= \underline{\qquad}$ halves

2. How many thirds are in each amount?

   a) $7\frac{1}{3} + 2\frac{1}{3}$

      $= \underline{\qquad}$ thirds $+ \underline{\qquad}$ thirds

      $= \underline{\qquad}$ thirds

   b) $8\frac{1}{3} - 2\frac{2}{3}$

      $= \underline{\qquad}$ thirds $- \underline{\qquad}$ thirds

      $= \underline{\qquad}$ thirds

3. Add or subtract. Write your answer two ways. One answer will be a whole number.

   a) $1\frac{3}{8} + 2\frac{4}{8} = \frac{11}{8} + \frac{20}{8}$

   b) $6\frac{7}{10} - 2\frac{4}{10} = \frac{\quad}{10} - \frac{\quad}{10}$

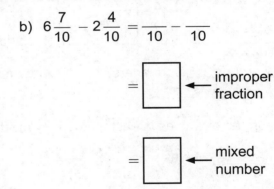

   $= \boxed{\dfrac{31}{8}} \longleftarrow$ improper fraction

   $= \boxed{3\frac{7}{8}} \longleftarrow$ mixed number

   $= \boxed{} \longleftarrow$ improper fraction

   $= \boxed{} \longleftarrow$ mixed number

   c) $1 + 5\frac{3}{4}$ d) $1\frac{5}{8} + 2\frac{3}{8}$ e) $6 - 2\frac{3}{5}$ f) $7\frac{1}{8} - 3\frac{4}{8}$

4. Rima needs $1\frac{2}{5}$ cups of flour to make a cake and 2 cups of flour to make a pizza. How much flour does she need altogether? $\underline{\qquad}$

5. Mike bought a rope $2\frac{1}{4}$ feet long. He cut off $\frac{3}{4}$ of a foot from it. How much rope is left? $\underline{\qquad}$

53. Equal Parts of a Set

Fractions can name parts of a set: $\frac{1}{5}$ of the figures are squares, $\frac{1}{5}$ are circles, and $\frac{3}{5}$ are triangles.

□ △ △ ○ △

1. Fill in the blanks.

a) ○ △ ○

   ☐ of the figures are circles.

   ☐ of the figures are shaded.

b) ☐ ☐ ☐ ○ △

   ☐ of the figures are shaded.

   ☐ of the figures are triangles.

2. ☐ △ △ ○ ☐ ☐ △ ☐

a) $\frac{4}{8}$ of the figures are _____.

b) $\frac{3}{8}$ of the figures are _____.

3. A soccer team wins 5 games and loses 3 games.

a) How many games did the team play? ☐

b) What fraction of the games did the team win? ☐

4. A box contains 4 blue markers, 3 black markers, and 3 red markers. What fraction of the markers are *not* blue?

5. Write four fraction statements for the picture: ☐ △ ☐ ○ ○

6. Draw a picture that fits all the clues.

a) There are 5 circles and squares.

   $\frac{3}{5}$ of the figures are squares.

   $\frac{2}{5}$ of the figures are shaded.

   Two circles are shaded.

b) There are 5 triangles and squares.

   $\frac{3}{5}$ of the figures are shaded.

   $\frac{2}{5}$ of the figures are triangles.

   One square is shaded.

54. Fractions of Whole Numbers

Dan has 6 cookies.

He wants to give $\frac{1}{3}$ of his cookies to a friend.

He makes 3 equal groups and gives 1 group to his friend.

There are 2 cookies in each group, so $\frac{1}{3}$ of 6 is 2.

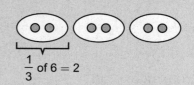

$\frac{1}{3}$ of 6 = 2

1. Use the picture to find the fraction of the number.

a)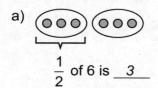

$\frac{1}{2}$ of 6 is ___3___

b)

$\frac{1}{3}$ of 12 is _____

c)

_____ of 8 is _____

d)

_____ of 8 is _____

Tia has 10 cookies. She wants to give $\frac{3}{5}$ of her cookies to a friend. She makes 5 equal groups and gives 3 of the groups to her friend.

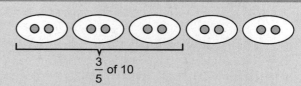

$\frac{3}{5}$ of 10

There are 2 in each group. So there are 6 in 3 groups. So $\frac{3}{5}$ of 10 is 6.

2. Circle the given amount.

a) $\frac{2}{3}$ of 6

b) $\frac{3}{4}$ of 8

c) $\frac{4}{5}$ of 10

d) $\frac{3}{4}$ of 12

3. Draw the correct number of dots in each group, and then circle the given amount.

a) $\frac{2}{3}$ of 12

b) $\frac{2}{3}$ of 9

4. Draw a picture to find $\frac{3}{4}$ of 12 cookies.

Gerome finds $\frac{1}{3}$ of 6 by dividing: 6 divided into 3 equal groups gives 2 in each group.

 $6 \div 3 = 2$ So $\frac{1}{3}$ of 6 is 2.

5. Find the fraction of the number. Write the division you used in the box.

a) $\frac{1}{2}$ of 8 = ___4___

$$8 \div 2$$

b) $\frac{1}{2}$ of 10 = _____

c) $\frac{1}{2}$ of 16 = _____

d) $\frac{1}{2}$ of 20 = _____

e) $\frac{1}{3}$ of 9 = _____

f) $\frac{1}{3}$ of 15 = _____

BONUS▶ $\frac{1}{1,000}$ of 4,000 = _____

6. Circle $\frac{1}{2}$ of each set of lines. Hint: Count the lines and divide by 2.

a) | | | | | |

b) | | | | | | | | | |

c) | | | | | | | | | | | | |

d) | | | | | | | | | | | | | |

7. Shade $\frac{1}{3}$ of the circles. Then circle $\frac{2}{3}$.

a)

b) ○○○○○○○○○○○○

c) ○○○

d) ○○○○○○○
○○○○○○

8. Shade $\frac{1}{4}$ of the triangles. Then circle $\frac{3}{4}$.

9. Shade $\frac{3}{5}$ of the boxes. Hint: First count the boxes and find $\frac{1}{5}$.

a)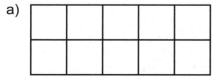

b)

Andy finds $\frac{2}{3}$ of 12 as follows:

Step 1: He finds $\frac{1}{3}$ of 12 by dividing 12 by 3:

(0000) (0000) (0000)

12 ÷ 3 = 4 (4 is $\frac{1}{3}$ of 12)

Step 2: He multiplies the result by 2:

(0000) (0000) (0000)

4 × 2 = 8 (8 is $\frac{2}{3}$ of 12)

10. Find the following amounts using Andy's method.

a) $\frac{2}{3}$ of 9

b) $\frac{3}{4}$ of 8

c) $\frac{2}{3}$ of 15

d) $\frac{2}{5}$ of 10

$\frac{1}{3}$ of 9 is _____

$\frac{1}{4}$ of 8 is _____

$\frac{1}{3}$ of 15 is _____

$\frac{1}{5}$ of 10 is _____

So $\frac{2}{3}$ of 9 is _____

So $\frac{3}{4}$ of 8 is _____

So $\frac{2}{3}$ of 15 is _____

So $\frac{2}{5}$ of 10 is _____

e) $\frac{3}{5}$ of 25

f) $\frac{2}{7}$ of 14

g) $\frac{1}{6}$ of 18

h) $\frac{1}{2}$ of 12

_____

_____

_____

_____

i) $\frac{3}{4}$ of 12

j) $\frac{2}{3}$ of 21

k) $\frac{3}{8}$ of 16

l) $\frac{3}{7}$ of 21

_____

_____

_____

_____

11. Five children are on a bus. $\frac{3}{5}$ are girls. How many girls are on the bus? _____

12. A pound of plums costs $8. How much would $\frac{3}{4}$ of a pound cost? _____

13. Gerald has 12 apples. He gave away $\frac{3}{4}$ of the apples. How many did he keep?

14. Ed studied for $\frac{2}{3}$ of an hour.

a) How many minutes did he study for? _____

b) Ed started studying at 7:10 p.m.
At what time did he stop studying? _____

c) Ed's favorite TV show starts at 8:00 p.m.
Did he finish studying before the show started? _____

55. Multiplying a Fraction by a Whole Number

Remember: You can multiply whole numbers on a number line.

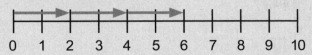

3 arrows of length 2 gives a total length of:

$$2 + 2 + 2 = 3 \times 2 = 6$$

You can multiply fractions on a number line too.

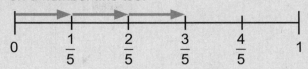

3 arrows of length $\frac{1}{5}$ gives a total length of:

$$\frac{1}{5} + \frac{1}{5} + \frac{1}{5} = 3 \times \frac{1}{5} = \frac{3}{5}$$

1. Multiply using the number line.

a)
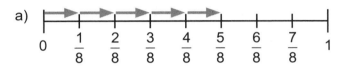

$$5 \times \frac{1}{8} =$$

b)

$$2 \times \frac{1}{5} =$$

c)
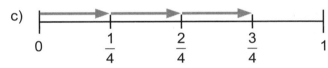

$$3 \times \frac{1}{4} =$$

d)
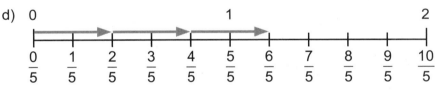

$$3 \times \frac{2}{5} = \frac{6}{5}$$

e)
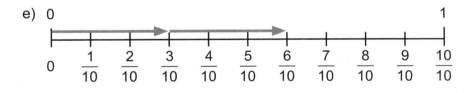

$$2 \times \frac{3}{10} =$$

2. Draw arrows above and below the number line to multiply the fraction.

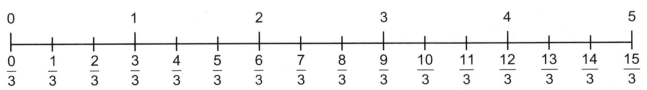

a) $2 \times \frac{4}{3} =$

b) $6 \times \frac{2}{3} =$

Sarah counts by $\frac{3}{8}$ to multiply $5 \times \frac{3}{8}$.

$\frac{3}{8}$ $\frac{6}{8}$ $\frac{9}{8}$ $\frac{12}{8}$ $\frac{15}{8}$ So $5 \times \frac{3}{8} = \frac{15}{8} = 1\frac{7}{8}$

3. Multiply by skip counting. Change your answer to a mixed number.

a) $5 \times \frac{3}{7}$ $\frac{3}{7}$, $\frac{6}{7}$, _____ , _____ , _____   So $5 \times \frac{3}{7} =$ _____ $=$ _____

b) $5 \times \frac{2}{9}$ _____ , _____ , _____ , _____ , _____   So $5 \times \frac{2}{9} =$ _____ $=$ _____

4. Multiply by adding.

a) $3 \times \frac{4}{5} = \frac{4}{5} + \frac{4}{5} + \frac{4}{5} =$

b) $4 \times \frac{5}{8} = \frac{5}{8} + \frac{5}{8} + \frac{5}{8} + \frac{5}{8} =$

c) $8 \times \frac{3}{7} = \frac{3}{7} + \frac{3}{7} + \frac{3}{7} + \frac{3}{7} + \frac{3}{7} + \frac{3}{7} + \frac{3}{7} + \frac{3}{7} =$

5. Multiply mentally.

a) $5 \times \frac{3}{8} = \frac{\boxed{15}}{8}$ ◄— 5×3

b) $4 \times \frac{2}{7} = \frac{\boxed{}}{7}$ ◄— 4×2

c) $2 \times \frac{4}{9} =$

d) $5 \times \frac{5}{9} =$

e) $3 \times \frac{5}{6} =$

f) $2 \times \frac{5}{3} =$

6. Multiply by changing the mixed number to an improper fraction.
    Write your answer two ways.

a) $4 \times 1\frac{2}{5} = 4 \times \boxed{}$

b) $2 \times 3\frac{1}{3} = 2 \times \boxed{}$

$= \boxed{}$ ◄— improper fraction

$= \boxed{}$ ◄— mixed number

$= \boxed{}$ ◄— improper fraction

$= \boxed{}$ ◄— mixed number

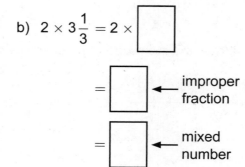

c) $3 \times 2\frac{1}{5}$

d) $5 \times 1\frac{3}{8}$

e) $7 \times 1\frac{4}{5}$

f) $2 \times 3\frac{5}{6}$

56. Problems and Puzzles

1. Five people each ate $\frac{1}{8}$ of a cake. Write an addition and a multiplication
    to show how much they ate altogether.

    Addition: _____   Multiplication: _____

2. Leo wants to make grilled cheese sandwiches for five people.
    Each person needs $\frac{3}{8}$ of a pound of cheese.

    a) How many pounds of cheese does he need? _____
        Hint: Use the picture to help.

    b) Leo has 2 pounds of cheese. Does he need to buy more cheese? _____

3. Latasha makes 5 batches of a pizza. Each batch needs $\frac{2}{3}$ cups of flour.

    a) How much flour will she need altogether? _____

    b) She has 4 cups of flour. How much flour will she have left? _____
        Hint: Shade the amount of flour she needs. How many thirds are not shaded?

    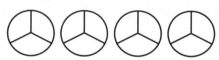

4. Lee makes 8 batches of cookies for a bake sale. Each batch needs $2\frac{3}{4}$ of a cup of flour.
    A cup of flour costs 30¢. How much does he have to pay for the flour?
    Write your answer in both cents and dollars.

5. Six people are having dinner together. Each person needs $\frac{3}{8}$ of a pound of turkey.

    a) How many pounds of turkey will be needed? ☐

    b) Between what two whole numbers does your answer lie? _____ and _____

6. Sarah says $3 \times 2\frac{1}{5} = 6\frac{3}{5}$ because $3 \times 2 = 6$ and $3 \times \frac{1}{5} = \frac{3}{5}$. Is she right?

    Draw a picture to help you decide.

7. Write $\frac{7}{8}$ as a sum of two or more fractions in at least five ways.

Example: $\frac{7}{8} = \frac{1}{8} + \frac{3}{8} + \frac{3}{8}$

8. Write $\frac{1}{2}$ as a sum of three or more fractions in at least five ways.

Hint: First write some fractions that are equivalent to $\frac{1}{2}$: $\frac{2}{4}$, $\frac{3}{6}$, $\frac{4}{8}$, and so on.

9. a) Tasha wants to pour the juice from these two containers into a third container that is the same size.
Will the container overflow?

b) Is $\frac{4}{5} + \frac{1}{3}$ greater than 1? How do you know?

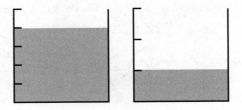

10. a) Tony had $\frac{2}{3}$ of a cup of juice. He drank $\frac{1}{3}$ of a *cup*.
Show on the picture how much he drank.
How much does he have left?

b) Alicia had $\frac{2}{3}$ of a cup of juice. She drank $\frac{1}{3}$ of the *juice*.
Use a ruler to show on the picture how much she drank.

c) Alicia says she has $\frac{1}{3}$ of a cup left because $\frac{2}{3} - \frac{1}{3} = \frac{1}{3}$.
Is she right? Explain.

Tony   **Alicia**

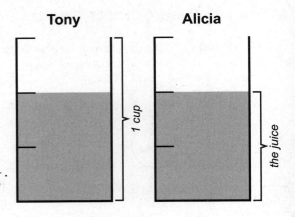

1 cup

the juice

11. A flower garden has 10 flowers.

$\frac{1}{2}$ of the flowers are lilies. $\frac{2}{5}$ of the flowers are daffodils.

a) How many lilies are in the garden?

b) How many daffodils are in the garden?

c) How many flowers are either lilies or daffodils?

d) Calculate $\frac{1}{2} + \frac{2}{5}$. Hint: Use your answer to part c).

BONUS ▶ How many more lilies are there than daffodils? Use your answer to calculate $\frac{1}{2} - \frac{2}{5}$.

57. Tenths and Hundredths (Fractions)

> A dime is $\frac{1}{10}$ of a dollar. A penny is $\frac{1}{100}$ of a dollar.

1. Write the fraction of a dollar the amount represents.

   a) 4 pennies ☐   b) 3 dimes ☐   c) 6 dimes ☐   d) 34 pennies ☐

2. Write how many pennies the dimes are worth. Then write a fraction equation.

   a) 3 dimes = __30__ pennies
   $$\frac{3}{10} = \frac{30}{100}$$

   b) 7 dimes = _____ pennies

   c) 8 dimes = _____ pennies

   d) 5 dimes = _____ pennies

3. Complete the table. The first row is done for you.

	Fraction of a Dollar (Tenths)	Number of Dimes	Number of Pennies	Fraction of a Dollar (Hundredths)
a)	$\frac{4}{10}$	4	40	$\frac{40}{100}$
b)		6		
c)			90	
d)	$\frac{3}{10}$			

4. Sarah says 37 pennies are worth more than 5 dimes because 37 coins are more than 5 coins. Is she right? Explain.

5. Shade the same amount in the second square. Then count by 10s to write the number of hundredths.

   a)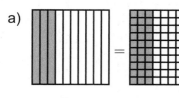
   $$\frac{3}{10} = \frac{}{100}$$

   b)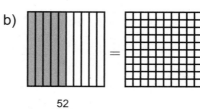
   $$\frac{52}{100} = \frac{}{100}$$

6. Count the columns to write the tenths. Count by 10s to write the hundredths.

a)

Picture	Tenths	Hundredths
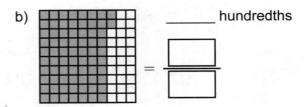	$\frac{2}{10}$	$\frac{20}{100}$

b)

Picture	Tenths	Hundredths

7. Count the number of hundredths. Write your answer two ways.
Hint: Count by tens and then by ones.

a) 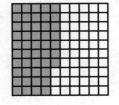   _____ hundredths

$= \frac{\boxed{}}{\boxed{}}$

b)   _____ hundredths

$= \frac{\boxed{}}{\boxed{}}$

8. Shade the fraction.

a) $\frac{47}{100}$

b) $\frac{3}{10}$

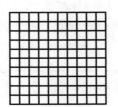

c) 5 hundredths

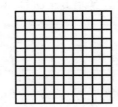

d) 4 tenths

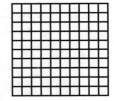

9. Shade the fraction. Then circle the greater fraction in each pair.

a) $\frac{38}{100}$ $\frac{6}{10}$

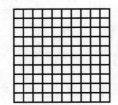   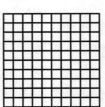

b) $\frac{4}{100}$ $\frac{7}{10}$

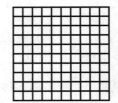   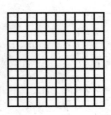

10. Rocco says that $\frac{17}{100}$ is greater than $\frac{8}{10}$ because 17 is greater than 8.

Is Rocco correct? Explain.

_____

_____

58. Decimal Tenths and Hundredths

A **tenth** (or $\frac{1}{10}$) can be represented in different ways.

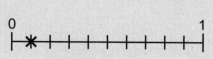

A tenth of the distance between 0 and 1

A tenth of a pie

A tenth of a hundreds block

A tenth of a tens block

Tenths commonly appear in units of measurement ("a millimeter is a tenth of a centimeter").

Mathematicians invented decimal tenths as a short form for tenths: $\frac{1}{10} = 0.1$, $\frac{2}{10} = 0.2$, and so on.

1. Write a fraction and a decimal for each shaded part in the boxes below.

a) $\frac{4}{10}$ 0.4

b)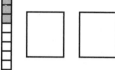

c)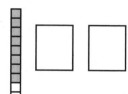

d)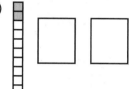

2. Write the decimal.

a) 5 tenths = __0.5__   b) 7 tenths = _____   c) 6 tenths = _____   d) 9 tenths = _____

3. Shade to show the decimal.

a) 0.3   b) 0.8   c) 0.5   d) 0.4

4. Show the decimal on the number line.

a) 0.8 of the distance from 0 to 1

b) 0.3 of the distance from 0 to 1

c) 0.5 of the distance from 0 to 1

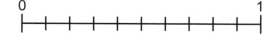

d) 0.9 of the distance from 0 to 1

A **hundredth** (or $\frac{1}{100}$) can be represented in different ways.

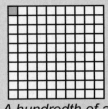

A hundredth of a hundreds block

0 ⊢⊢⊢⊢⊢⊢⊢⊢⊢⊢⊢⊢⊢⊢⊢⊢⊢⊢⊢⊢⊢⊢⊢⊢⊢⊢⊢⊢ 1

A hundredth of the distance from 0 to 1

Mathematicians invented decimal hundredths as a short form for hundredths.

Examples: $\frac{1}{100} = 0.01$, $\frac{8}{100} = 0.08$, $\frac{37}{100} = 0.37$

5. Write a fraction for the shaded part of the hundreds block. Then write the fraction as a decimal.
   Hint: Count by 10s for each column or row that is shaded.

   a) $\frac{60}{100} = 0.60$

   b)

   c)

   d)

   e)

   BONUS ▶

6. Write the decimal hundredths.

   a) 18 hundredths = _____   b) 9 hundredths = _____   c) 90 hundredths = _____

REMINDER ▶ Points farther to the right on a number line represent greater numbers.

Example: 5 is to the right of 3 because 5 > 3.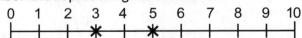

---

7. a) Show the decimals on the number line.

   A. 0.24   **B.** 0.70   **C.** 0.06   **D.** 0.45

   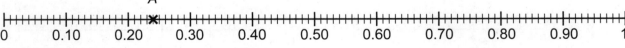

   b) Write the decimals in part a) from least to greatest.

   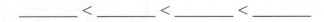

   _____ < _____ < _____ < _____

59. Comparing Decimal Tenths and Hundredths

1. Shade the same amount in the second square. Then count by 10s to find the number of hundredths. Write your answer as a fraction and a decimal.

a)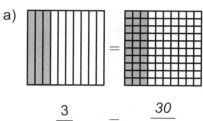

$$\frac{3}{10} = \frac{30}{100}$$

$$0.3 = \underline{0.30}$$

b)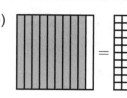

$$\frac{9}{10} = \frac{}{100}$$

$$0.9 = \underline{}$$

c)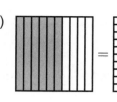

$$\frac{6}{10} = \frac{}{100}$$

$$0.6 = \underline{}$$

2. a) Complete the table. The first row is done for you.

	Fraction Tenths	Fraction Hundredths	Picture	Decimal Tenths	Decimal Hundredths
i)	$\frac{2}{10}$	$\frac{20}{100}$		0.2	0.20
ii)					
iii)					

b) Use part a) to write the decimals from smallest to greatest: 0.40   0.2   0.7

_____ < _____ < _____

3. Write how many tenths and how many hundredths. Then write an equation with decimals.

```
0           A                          B      C              1
|+++++++++|++++++*+++++|+++++++++|+++++++++|+++++*+++*++++|+++++++++|++++++++++|
```

A. _____ tenths   B. _____ tenths   C. _____ tenths

= _____ hundredths   = _____ hundredths   = _____ hundredths

So _____ = _____   So _____ = _____   So _____ = _____

4. Show the decimals on the number line. Then write the decimals from least to greatest.

a) **A.** 0.40   **B.** 0.05   **C.** 0.27

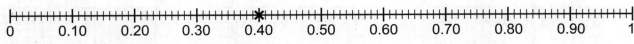

_____ < _____ < _____

b) **A.** 0.80   **B.** 0.08   **C.** 0.05

_____ < _____ < _____

5. Write the decimal as a fraction with denominator 100.

a) $0.7 = \dfrac{}{10} = \dfrac{}{100}$
b) $0.48 = \dfrac{}{100}$
c) $0.09 = \dfrac{}{100}$
d) $0.3 =$

6. Write the fraction as a decimal with 2 digits after the decimal point.

a) $\dfrac{6}{10} = 0.\underline{\quad}$
$= 0.\underline{\quad}\,\underline{\quad}$
b) $\dfrac{77}{100} = 0.\underline{\quad}\,\underline{\quad}$
c) $\dfrac{3}{10} = 0.\underline{\quad}$
$= 0.\underline{\quad}\,\underline{\quad}$
d) $\dfrac{9}{100} = 0.\underline{\quad}\,\underline{\quad}$

7. Circle the equalities that are incorrect.

$0.52 = \dfrac{52}{100}$ $0.8 = \dfrac{8}{10}$ $\dfrac{17}{100} = 0.17$ $\dfrac{3}{100} = 0.03$

$0.7 = \dfrac{7}{100}$ $0.53 = \dfrac{53}{100}$ $0.05 = \dfrac{5}{100}$ $0.02 = \dfrac{2}{10}$

8. Write the decimals as hundredths to compare the decimals. Then write < or >.

a) 0.4   0.73
b) 0.2   0.16
c) 0.7   0.59

$= \dfrac{}{100}$ $= \dfrac{}{100}$ $=$ $=$ $=$ $=$

0.4 ☐ 0.73   0.2 ☐ 0.16   0.7 ☐ 0.59

JUMP Math Accumula

60. Combining Tenths and Hundredths

1. Describe the shaded fraction in four ways.

a)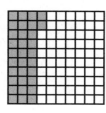

_32_ hundredths = _3_ tenths _2_ hundredths

$$\frac{32}{100} = 0.\ \underline{3}\ \underline{2}$$

b)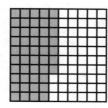

____ hundredths = ___ tenths ___ hundredths

$$\frac{}{100} = 0.\ \underline{}\ \underline{}$$

c)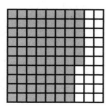

____ hundredths = ___ tenths ___ hundredths

$$\frac{}{100} = 0.\ \underline{}\ \underline{}$$

d)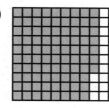

____ hundredths = ___ tenths ___ hundredths

$$\frac{}{100} = 0.\ \underline{}\ \underline{}$$

2. Fill in the blanks.

a) 71 hundredths = _7_ tenths _1_ hundredth

$$\frac{71}{100} = 0.\ \underline{7}\ \underline{1}$$

b) 28 hundredths = ____ tenths ____ hundredths

$$\frac{}{100} = 0.\ \underline{}\ \underline{}$$

c) 41 hundredths = ____ tenths ____ hundredth

$$\frac{}{100} = 0.\ \underline{}\ \underline{}$$

d) 60 hundredths = ____ tenths ____ hundredths

$$\frac{}{100} = 0.\ \underline{}\ \underline{}$$

e) 8 hundredths = ____ tenths ____ hundredths

$$\frac{}{100} = 0.\ \underline{}\ \underline{}$$

f) 2 hundredths = ____ tenths ____ hundredths

$$\frac{}{100} = 0.\ \underline{}\ \underline{}$$

3. Describe each decimal in two ways.

a) 0.52 = _5_ tenths _2_ hundredths

= _52 hundredths_

b) 0.83 = ____ tenths ____ hundredths

= _____

c) 0.70 = ____ tenths ____ hundredths

= _____

d) 0.02 = ____ tenths ____ hundredths

= _____

Sohrab describes the distance covered on a number line in two ways.

43 hundredths = 4 tenths 3 hundredths

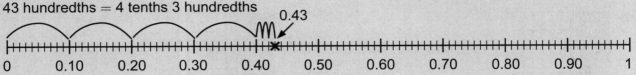

0   0.10   0.20   0.30   0.40   0.50   0.60   0.70   0.80   0.90   1

4. Write the distance covered in two ways.

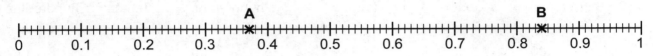

0   0.1   0.2   0.3   0.4   0.5   0.6   0.7   0.8   0.9   1

A. ____ tenths ____ hundredths   **B.** ____ tenths ____ hundredths

= ____ hundredths   = ____ hundredths

5. Estimate and mark the location of the decimals on the number line.

a) **A.** 0.62   **B.** 0.35   **C.** 0.99

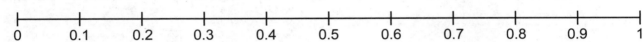

0   0.1   0.2   0.3   0.4   0.5   0.6   0.7   0.8   0.9   1

b) **A.** 0.37   **B.** 0.28   **C.** 0.51

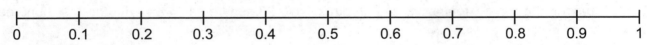

0   0.1   0.2   0.3   0.4   0.5   0.6   0.7   0.8   0.9   1

REMINDER ▶ A meter is 100 centimeters.

6. What part of a meter is the length shown? Write your answer as a decimal and a fraction.

a)

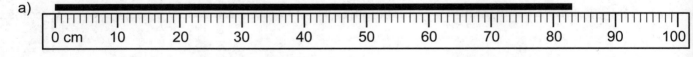

0 cm   10   20   30   40   50   60   70   80   90   100

83 cm = ___0.83___ m = $\dfrac{83}{100}$ m

b)

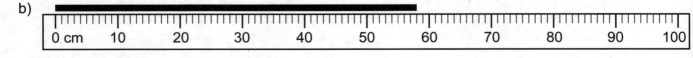

0 cm   10   20   30   40   50   60   70   80   90   100

58 cm = _____ m = ☐ m

61. Decimals and Money

A **dime** is **one tenth** of a dollar. A **penny** is **one hundredth** of a dollar.

1. Express the value of each decimal in four different ways.

   a) 0.73

       7 dimes 3 pennies

       7 tenths 3 hundredths

       73 pennies

       73 hundredths

   b) 0.62

   c) 0.48

   d) 0.03

   e) 0.09

   f) 0.19

2. Express the value of the decimal in four different ways.

   a) 0.6 _____ dimes _____ pennies

        _____ tenths _____ hundredths

        _____ pennies

        _____ hundredths

   b) 0.8 _____ dimes _____ pennies

        _____ tenths _____ hundredths

        _____ pennies

        _____ hundredths

3. Express the value of each decimal in four different ways. Then circle the greater number.

   0.3 _____ dimes _____ pennies

        _____ tenths _____ hundredths

        _____ pennies

        _____ hundredths

   0.18 _____ dimes _____ pennies

        _____ tenths _____ hundredths

        _____ pennies

        _____ hundredths

4. Will says 0.32 is greater than 0.5 because 32 is greater than 5. Can you explain his mistake?

62. Adding Tenths and Hundredths

1. Write the fraction addition for each statement.
   Hint: Replace "is the same amount of money as" with the equal sign (=).

   a) 1 dime and 2 pennies is the same amount of money as 12 pennies.

   $$\frac{1}{10} + \frac{2}{100} = \frac{12}{100}$$

   b) 3 dimes and 4 pennies is the same amount of money as 34 pennies.

   c) 2 dimes and 5 pennies is the same amount of money as _____ pennies.

2. Shade the total. Then write a fraction addition. Hint: Count by 10s for the columns you shaded.

   a)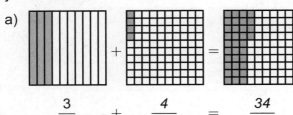

   $$\frac{3}{10} + \frac{4}{100} = \frac{34}{100}$$

   b)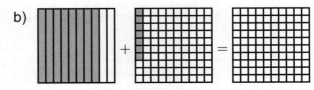

   c)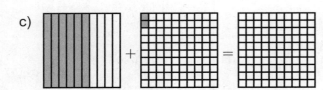

   d)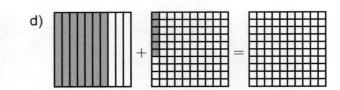

3. Shade the total. Then write a decimal addition.

   a)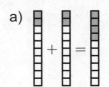

   b)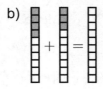

   c)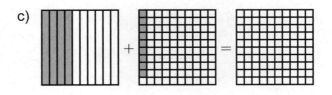

   $\underline{\quad 0.2 + 0.2 = 0.4 \quad}$ $\underline{\hspace{3cm}}$ $\underline{\hspace{4cm}}$

To add $\dfrac{3}{10} + \dfrac{4}{100}$:

Step 1: Change the tenths to hundredths. $\dfrac{3 \times 10}{10 \times 10} = \dfrac{30}{100}$

Step 2: Add the hundredths. $\dfrac{30}{100} + \dfrac{4}{100} = \dfrac{34}{100}$

4. Write an equivalent fraction with denominator 100.

   a) $\dfrac{8}{10} = \dfrac{}{100}$

   b) $\dfrac{7}{10} = \dfrac{}{100}$

   c) $\dfrac{4}{10} =$

   d) $\dfrac{3}{10} =$

5. Add the hundredths.

   a) $\dfrac{20}{100} + \dfrac{3}{100}$

   b) $\dfrac{40}{100} + \dfrac{5}{100}$

   c) $\dfrac{70}{100} + \dfrac{2}{100}$

   d) $\dfrac{60}{100} + \dfrac{8}{100}$

   $= \dfrac{}{100}$

   $=$

   $=$

   $=$

6. Add the tenths and hundredths.

   a) $\dfrac{52}{100} + \dfrac{3}{100}$

   b) $\dfrac{3}{10} + \dfrac{7}{100}$

   c) $\dfrac{9}{10} + \dfrac{2}{100}$

   BONUS ▶ $\dfrac{7}{10} + \dfrac{15}{100}$

   $= \dfrac{}{100} + \dfrac{}{100}$

   $= \dfrac{}{100} + \dfrac{}{100}$

   $=$

   $=$

   $= \dfrac{}{100}$

   $= \dfrac{}{100}$

   $=$

   $=$

7. Add mentally.

   a) $\dfrac{7}{10} + \dfrac{4}{100} = \dfrac{}{100}$

   b) $\dfrac{6}{10} + \dfrac{9}{100} =$

   c) $\dfrac{1}{10} + \dfrac{9}{100} =$

   BONUS ▶ $\dfrac{8}{10} + \dfrac{13}{100} =$

8. Tyrell has $\dfrac{4}{10}$ of a dollar and Tania has $\dfrac{7}{100}$ of a dollar. What fraction of a dollar do they have altogether?

9. A snail crawled $\dfrac{3}{10}$ of a meter, and then crawled another $\dfrac{9}{100}$ of a meter. What fraction of a meter did the snail crawl altogether?

BONUS ▶ Abdi biked $\dfrac{7}{10}$ km on Monday and $\dfrac{29}{100}$ km on Tuesday. Did he bike more than a kilometer?

63. Decimals Greater Than 1

> A mixed number can be written as a decimal.
>
> Examples: $12\dfrac{3}{10} = 12.3$ $2\dfrac{85}{100} = 2.85$
>
> The decimal point separates the whole number part (on the left) and the fraction part (on the right).

1. Write the mixed number as a decimal.

   a) $3\dfrac{4}{10} = $ _____

   b) $12\dfrac{52}{100} = $ _____

   c) $8\dfrac{45}{100} = $ _____

   d) $46\dfrac{3}{100} = $ _____

> **REMINDER ▶**
>
> The number of digits to the right of the decimal point = the number of zeros in the denominator
>
> Examples: $3.45 = 3\dfrac{45}{100}$ $34.5 = 34\dfrac{5}{10}$ $34.05 = 34\dfrac{5}{100}$

2. Write the denominator of the fraction part for the equivalent mixed number.

   a) 4.9 _____

   b) 1.58 _____

   c) 15.08 _____

   BONUS ▶ 18.3402 _____

3. Write the decimal as a mixed number.

   a) 3.81 =

   b) 6.9 =

   c) 7.04 =

   d) 18.15 =

   e) 13.4 =

   f) 17.06 =

   g) 193.45 =

   BONUS ▶ 7.004 =

> You can write a decimal in words. Use "and" for the decimal point.
>
> Examples: $12\dfrac{3}{10} = 12.3 = $ twelve **and** three tenths $2\dfrac{85}{100} = 2.85 = $ two **and** eighty-five hundredths

4. Write "tenths" or "hundredths." Hint: Count the digits to the right of the decimal point.

   a) 3.12 = three and twelve _____

   b) 18.7 = eighteen and seven _____

   c) 6.05 = six and five _____

   d) 20.8 = twenty and eight _____

5. Write the equivalent words or decimal.

   a) 7.4 = _____

   b) 4.09 = _____

   c) seventy-four and eleven hundredths = _____

   d) twenty and four tenths = _____

Example: $\dfrac{28}{10}$

$28 \div 10 = 2 \text{ R } 8$, so $\dfrac{28}{10} = 2\dfrac{8}{10}$

6. Change the improper fraction to a mixed number.

a) $\dfrac{74}{10}$ $74 \div 10 =$ _____ R _____

     So $\dfrac{74}{10} =$

b) $\dfrac{684}{100}$ $684 \div 100 =$ _____ R _____

     So $\dfrac{684}{100} =$

7. Change the improper fraction to a mixed number and then to a decimal.

a) $\dfrac{35}{10} = 3\dfrac{5}{10} = 3.5$

b) $\dfrac{387}{100} = 3\dfrac{87}{100} = 3.87$

c) $\dfrac{41}{10} =$

d) $\dfrac{642}{10} =$

e) $\dfrac{564}{100} =$

f) $\dfrac{4,208}{100} =$

8. Write the decimal as an improper fraction with denominator 10 or 100.

a) $3.8 =$ b) $7.08 =$ c) $8.60 =$ d) $60.04 =$

e) $70.8 =$ f) $17.5 =$ g) $31.89 =$ h) $90.4 =$

Remember: $\dfrac{8}{10} = \dfrac{80}{100}$ So $2\dfrac{8}{10} = 2\dfrac{80}{100}$ So $2.8 = 2.80$

9. Complete the tables. Part a) is done for you.

	Decimal Tenths	Fraction Tenths	Fraction Hundredths	Decimal Hundredths
a)	2.7	$\dfrac{27}{10}$	$\dfrac{270}{100}$	2.70
b)	3.8			
c)	3.9			
d)	6.4			

	Decimal Tenths	Fraction Tenths	Fraction Hundredths	Decimal Hundredths
e)	59.4			
f)		$\dfrac{75}{10}$		
g)			$\dfrac{670}{100}$	
h)				30.80

64. Different Wholes (Advanced)

1. Write the fraction and the decimal.

   a) What fraction of a dime is a penny?

   A penny is worth _____ dimes.

   b) What fraction of a dollar is a penny?

   A penny is worth _____ dollars.

2. a) Hiro has pennies worth 0.5 dimes. How many pennies does he have? _____

   b) Naomi has pennies worth 0.5 dollars. How many pennies does she have? _____

   c) Who has more pennies? _____

3. a) Adam has pennies worth 0.4 dimes. How many pennies does he have? _____

   b) Rashida has pennies worth 0.25 dollars. How many pennies does she have? _____

   c) Who has more pennies? _____

   d) Rashida thinks 0.25 is more than 0.4 because she has more money.
      Is she correct? Explain.

   _____

   _____

4. Sarah says 0.25 is more than 0.3 because more is shaded. Is she right? Explain.

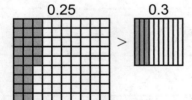

0.25   0.3

_____

_____

_____

5. Is it possible for 0.3 of one square to be more than 0.4 of another square?
   Show your thinking with a picture.

6. Is it possible for 0.3 on one number line to be farther right than 0.5 on another number line?
   Show your thinking with a picture.

65. Problems and Puzzles

1. Add and then write the equation in decimal form.

   a) $3 + \dfrac{24}{100} = 3\dfrac{24}{100}$ b) $2 + \dfrac{8}{10} =$ c) $5 + \dfrac{7}{100} =$ d) $9 + \dfrac{53}{100} =$

   $3 + 0.24 = 3.24$

2. Write how many tenths are in each number. Then add and subtract.

   $2.3 =$ _____ tenths and $1.4 =$ _____ tenths.   So $2.3 + 1.4$ $2.3 - 1.4$

   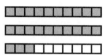   

   $=$ _____ tenths $=$ _____ tenths

   $= \dfrac{}{10}$ $= \dfrac{}{10}$

   $=$ _____ . _____ $=$ _____ . _____

3. a) Write three decimal hundredths between 0.3 and 0.4. _____, _____, _____

   b) Add 5 to your answers to part a). _____, _____, _____
      Hint: Use the pattern you observed in your answers to Question 1.

   c) Your answers to part b) are between what two tenths? _____ and _____

4. a) How many cents are in 3 dollars? __300__

      How many cents are in 3 dollars and 8 cents? __308__

   b) How many centimeters are in 3 meters? _____

      How many centimeters are in 3 meters and 8 centimeters? _____

   c) How many ounces are in 3 pounds? _____

      How many ounces are in 3 pounds and 8 ounces? _____

   d) What is more like cents: centimeters or ounces? Explain.

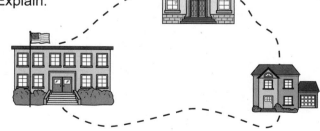

5. Gia biked 2 km to school, $\dfrac{8}{10}$ km to the library, and then $2\dfrac{9}{100}$ km home. How far did Gia bike altogether?

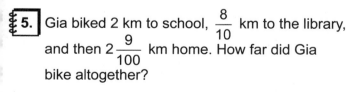

6. Miguel has red, blue, and yellow marbles. $\dfrac{7}{10}$ are red and $\dfrac{6}{100}$ are blue. What fraction is yellow?